SpringerBriefs in Criminology

Policing

Series Editor

M. R. Haberfeld
City University of New York
John Jay College of Criminal Justice
New York, NY, USA

D1806689

SpringerBriefs in Criminology present concise summaries of cutting edge research across the fields of Criminology and Criminal Justice. It publishes small but impactful volumes of between 50-125 pages, with a clearly defined focus. The series covers a broad range of Criminology research from experimental design and methods, to brief reports and regional studies, to policy-related applications.

The scope of the series spans the whole field of Criminology and Criminal Justice, with an aim to be on the leading edge and continue to advance research. The series will be international and cross-disciplinary, including a broad array of topics, including juvenile delinquency, policing, crime prevention, terrorism research, crime and place, quantitative methods, experimental research in criminology, research design and analysis, forensic science, crime prevention, victimology, criminal justice systems, psychology of law, and explanations for criminal behavior.

SpringerBriefs in Criminology will be of interest to a broad range of researchers and practitioners working in Criminology and Criminal Justice Research and in related academic fields such as Sociology, Psychology, Public Health, Economics and Political Science.

More information about this series at http://www.springer.com/series/10159

Frank S. Pezzella • Matthew D. Fetzer

The Measurement of Hate Crimes in America

 Springer

Frank S. Pezzella
Department of Criminal Justice
John Jay College of Criminal Justice
New York City, NY, USA

Matthew D. Fetzer
Department of Criminal Justice
Shippensburg University
Shippensburg, PA, USA

ISSN 2192-8533   ISSN 2192-8541   (electronic)
SpringerBriefs in Criminology
ISSN 2194-6213   ISSN 2194-6221   (electronic)
SpringerBriefs in Policing
ISBN 978-3-030-51576-8   ISBN 978-3-030-51577-5   (eBook)
https://doi.org/10.1007/978-3-030-51577-5

This Springer imprint is published by the registered company Springer Nature Switzerland AG
The registered company address is: Gewerbestrasse 11, 6330 Cham, Switzerland

Contents

Author Biographies

Frank S. Pezzella (Criminal Justice, SUNY Albany) is an Associate Professor in the Department of Criminal Justice at John Jay College of Criminal Justice and the Program of Doctoral Studies in Criminal Justice at the Graduate Center of the City University of New York. He is the author of *Hate Crime Statutes: A Public Policy and Law Enforcement Dilemma*, a Springer brief about the policy dilemmas and unintended consequences of hate crime statutes. Frank is the coauthor of several research reports that delineate the prevalence and severity of injuries to hate crime victims. He regularly teaches undergraduate and graduate courses about hate crime offending and victimizations.

Matthew D. Fetzer (Criminal Justice, SUNY Albany) is an Associate Professor in the Department of Criminal Justice at Shippensburg University. His research interests include the measurement of crime and delinquency, hate crime, violence, and juvenile justice. Prior to his current position, he worked as a Program Research Specialist for the New York State Division of Criminal Justice Services. While working for New York State, he first began conducting research on hate crime in addition to topics of homicide and domestic violence.

Chapter 1
Hate Crime Legislation and Jurisprudence

Abstract This chapter summarizes the problems with measuring the prevalence and severity hate crimes in the United States that are delineated in greater detail in later chapters. The chapter explains the various types of contemporary hate crime legislation with a focus on their similarities and differences and ramifications for accurately measuring the prevalence of hate crimes. The chapter examines federal and state variations in statutory provisions with particular emphasis on differences in statutorily protected bias groups and evidentiary criteria. This chapter focuses in some detail on evidentiary criteria including discriminatory selection, animus, "because of" and "by reason of" evidentiary standards. The chapter also summarizes landmark supreme court decisions that have set the legal parameters for the promulgation of federal and state hate crime statutes within the constitutional constraints of the First and Fourteenth Amendments. This chapter concludes with a discussion of the importance of accurate measurement as it relates to enacting evidence-based policies and practices that serve the most vulnerable and likely victims of hate crimes.

Keywords Contemporary hate crime legislation · Hate crime jurisprudence · Discriminatory selection statutes · Animus statutes · "Because of" "by reason of" statutes · Statutorily protected bias groups · Hate crime evidentiary standards · Civil remedies for hate crimes

Perhaps the largest obstacle to developing evidenced-based hate crime policies that serve the most victims throughout the United States is the erroneous estimation of its prevalence. Hate crime scholars and criminal justice practitioners for decades have lamented the underestimation of the prevalence of hate crimes. However, in the year 2020, 30 years after the promulgation of the Hate Crime Statistics Act (HCSA) of 1990, there is still no reliable method for estimating the scope of hate crimes. Arguably, in this data driven age, hate crime offending is perhaps one of very few crimes that have initiated a groundswell of statutes based on an incomplete

© The Author(s), under exclusive license to Springer Nature Switzerland
AG 2021
F. S. Pezzella, M. D. Fetzer, *The Measurement of Hate Crimes in America*,
SpringerBriefs in Criminology, https://doi.org/10.1007/978-3-030-51577-5_1

understanding of the scope and severity of hate crimes that occur each year. Today, a plethora of state statutes have been enacted that vary significantly in severity of sanctions, evidentiary criteria and statutorily defined protected groups. Consequently, a victim of a hate crime in one state may not have a cause of action in another. Yet, the hate crime offenders' bias motivation in both states may be identical. That is, hate crime offenders may similarly choose their victims not because of who they are, but what they are or what they represent (Lawrence, 1999).

Opponents of hate crime statutes contend hate crime policy and statutes are driven more by identity politics (Jacobs & Potter, 1998; Chakraborti & Garland, 2012). Others argue that victim groups that have the best advocacy efforts may be more likely to attain special protection under federal and state hate crime statutes (Grattet & Jenness, 2001; Mallett, Huntsinger, & Swim, 2011; Chakraborti & Garland, 2012). In addition, heinous types of hate crime victimizations that have come to the attention of the public have an impact on the construction of hate crime policy and statutes. Tragic incidents like the 2014 shooting of three perceived Jewish people outside of a Jewish community center by Frazier Glen Miller, the 2015 shooting of African American worshippers at the Mother Emanuel African Methodist Episcopal church by Dylan Roof, or the 2017 vehicular homicide killing of Heather Heyer at the far right rally in Charlottesville, Virginia have certainly raised the consciousness of the public about the problem of hate crimes. However, we think that constructing hate crime policy and statutes based on isolated incidents is more of a knee jerk reaction to the public's outcry. Hate crime scholars readily concede that mission offenders such as those that perpetrated the atrocities mentioned above represent only about 1% of all hate crimes (McDevitt, Levin, & Bennett, 2002; Pezzella, 2017). Generally, hate crimes offenses perpetrated by defensive, retaliatory, and thrill-seeking offenders occur much more frequently but are not necessarily nearly as lethal (McDevitt et al., 2002). Though less lethal, they are still quite detrimental to victims and society at large. However, to develop a hate crime policy that serves the majority of victims, we need to first understand the prevalence and severity of hate crimes and the bias motivations and types that prompt these attacks.

Several questions remain unanswered and continue to confound researchers and policymakers. How much hate crime is there? Is it increasing or decreasing? How severe is the problem? To whom does it impact most? How severe are the injuries? These questions cannot presently be answered accurately because our data is incomplete. Annual FBI hate crime estimates have already been conceded as largely inaccurate (Comey, 2014). For example, the Bureau of Justice Statistics (BJS) estimates more than 200,000 hate crimes per year as perceived by victims; however, the FBI data suggest an average of 8000 incidents per year (Masucci & Langton, 2017). Some researchers assert there is huge dark figure of underreporting (Pezzella, Fetzer, & Keller, 2019). Explanations for the underreporting of hate crimes and the lack of consistency between the two official reports of hate crimes will be explained in Chaps. 7 and 8.

Our goal in writing this book is to identify the measurement problems that have led to the underestimation of hate crime offending. We believe the real work in developing an evidence-based hate crime policy begins first by building a framework for the accurate measurement of hate crimes. We think that unpacking the problems that impede the accurate measurement of hate crimes will lead to data driven policies that coincide with the needs of primary and secondary victims. To these ends, we present the landscape of hate crime offending and the issues that confound its measurement.

Contemporary Hate Crime Legislation

Hate crime legislation is a broad, rather general term that represents a host of provisions not always discussed under the rubric of hate crime. In the year 2020, the number of hate crime statutory provisions and participating police agencies in the federal hate crime reporting program has expanded substantially with a diversity of purposes of hate crime legislation. For instance, 44 states have enacted institutional vandalism lawsuits; 32 states have promulgated civil action lawsuits; 25 states legislatively authorized hate crime data collection statutes; 25 states have enacted cross burning statutes; and 15 states incorporated statutory police training provisions (ADL, 2019). The emergence of hate crime legislation and its diverse provisions is relatively unprecedented in history. However, history informs us that the legacy of hate crimes in the United States has a long and sordid past despite numerous legislative and judicial attempts over centuries to proscribe hate-motivated violence (Levin, 2002). In the nineteenth and twentieth centuries numerous Reconstruction Era and Civil Rights legislation was enacted to outlaw hate motivated violence against African Americans. However, in this brief, we address the problems of measuring hate crimes since the promulgation of modern hate crime legislation by federal and state governments.

We conceptualized the origin of contemporary hate crime legislation with the promulgation of the Hate Crime Statistic Act (HCSA) of 1990. The HCSA authorized the attorney general to facilitate collection of hate crime data from voluntary police agencies throughout the country. Primarily a data collection statute, the HCSA was enacted without enforcement powers. However, between 1990 and 2019, Congress and the states enacted legislation that expanded enforcement power and jurisdiction for bias-related crimes. Contemporary hate crime legislation adopted by the federal and states governments has origins in the ADL's model hate crime legislation. The ADL model proposed four main legislative responses to bias crimes: (1) institutional vandalism, a special statutory law for property crime against cemeteries and other religious institutions; (2) enhanced penalties for offenders who commit bias crimes; (3) civil action, allowing for law suits against attackers; and (4) requirements for law enforcement training and data collection (ADL, 2012).

Table 1.1 displays the federal hate crime legislation that has been enacted since the promulgation of the HCSA. Note that subsequent legislation continues to expand enforcement powers, jurisdiction, and the number of protected bias

Table 1.1 Contemporary hate crime legislation

Year	U.S. Code	Legislative Intent
1990	28 U.S.C.§ 534	**Hate Crime Statistics Act** – voluntary police collection of hate crime data
1994	28 U.S.C. § 994	**Hate Crime Sentencing Enhancement Act** – authority for U.S. Sentencing Commission to enhance penalties for hate crime convictions by no less than three offense levels
1994	42 U.S.C. § 13701	**The Violence Against Women Act** – provided that all persons shall be free of crimes of violence motivated by gender
1996	18 U.S.C. § 247	**The Church Arson Prevention Act of 1996** – proscribed interference with exercise of religious belief and destruction of property
1998	20 U.S.C. § 1092 (f) (1) (F)	**Higher Education Act** – amendment authorized college campuses to collect hate crime data.
2008	H.R. § 351	**Emmett Till Unsolved Civil Rights Act** – authorizes investigation and prosecution of civil rights era racially motivated murders
2009	18 U.S.C. § 249	**Matthew Shepard & James Byrd Jr. Hate Crime Prevention Act** – expanded federal jurisdiction and protected categories to include disability, gender and gender identity.
2019	18 U.S. § 242	**Justice for Victims of Lynching Act** – amendment to include lynching as a federal criminal civil rights violation and a hate crime subject to enhanced penalties

categories. Perhaps one of the more unique aspects of contemporary hate crimes legislation that distinguishes it from civil rights era statutes is the increasing number of protected bias categories. Contemporary hate crime legislation typically extends protection beyond the original civil rights categories of race, religion, color, or national origin to sexual orientation, gender, disability and other bias categories. For instance, the federal hate crime statute, 18 U.S. § 249 (2009), increased the number of bias categories from actual or perceived race, color, religion, national origin, and sexual orientation to include gender, gender-identity, and disability status. In addition, 45 states have also enacted hate crime legislation although they vary significantly in statutorily protected bias categories and evidentiary requirements for prosecution (ADL, 2019). Jenness and Broad (1997) explain the burgeoning number of bias categories as a result of successful mobilization by advocacy groups such as the Anti-Defamation League (ADL), the Southern Poverty law Center (SPLC), and the National Gay and Lesbian Taskforce (NGLT). The plethora of federal and state legislation enacted since the HCSA indicates a recognition of the unique harm of hate crime. However, the variation in statutory construction of these statutes reflects different conceptualizations of what constitutes a hate crime. Some states provide statutory protection for bias categories that others do not. Similarly, the burden of evidence required to constitute a hate crime varies significantly across the states and the federal government. Consequently, estimating accurate counts largely depends on how you define a hate crime. We think the variation in state and federal statutorily protected bias categories and evidence standards hampers our ability to accurately estimate the frequency and severity of hate crimes.

Variation in Statutorily Protected Groups

A major obstacle to understanding the extent of hate crime in the United States is the inability to reconcile the differences in statutorily protected bias categories across the states. At the present time, the federal government recognizes hates crimes against persons because of their race, ethnicity, religion, disability, sexual orientation, gender, and gender identity. States are free to diverge from the federal government regarding which groups are recognized as protected under their hate crime legislation, or they may not even have hate crime legislation. In many cases, this divergence is in the form of less coverage – fewer groups recognized as protected in comparison to the federal government. Of the states with hate crime legislation specifying categories of bias motivation 45 states recognize race, religion, and ethnicity; 32 recognize disability; 31 recognize sexual orientation; 31 recognize gender; and 18 recognize gender identity (ADL, 2019).[1] Furthermore, the ADL shows that only 15 states recognize all of the same categories identified by the federal government. Sometimes states will deviate in the opposite direction and include additional groups under their hate crime legislation that are not currently recognized by the federal government. The Anti-Defamation League (ADL) has identified 18 states that recognize additional groups as protected; some of which include national origin, political affiliation, age, homeless persons, military personnel, and first responders (ADL, 2019).

In review of hate crime legislation, there is no steadfast rule or uniform rationale employed in determining which groups are recognized as protected by statute. This is evident by those groups that are included in hate crime statutes across the country, and by those groups that are not included. Groups that are recognized and protected under hate crime legislation have, for the most part, been groups which have been historically targeted for crimes motivated by bias. Two traditional examples would include African Americans or Jewish persons. Other groups that have been legally identified as protected groups do not necessarily have as long of a history of being targeted, but they have a history nonetheless. Transgendered persons would be an illustration of such a group. The one common theme for group inclusion in hate crime statutes appears to be an identifiable history of targeting group members because of bias, and the reflected agreement by legislators to include these groups under hate crime laws. It is the latter that explains the significant variation in which groups are recognized by hate crime statutes across this country.

The net effect of the variation in statutorily protected groups makes it nearly impossible to estimate the true prevalence of bias crime. Clearly, what is defined as a bias crime in one state may not be in another. Moreover, the federal definition under 18 U.S. § 249 arguably limits the scope to those federally defined categories

---

[1] Arkansas, Georgia, South Carolina, and Wyoming do not have hate crime laws. Indiana passed hate crime legislation in 2019, but the language used in the statute did not specify any bias motivation categories (ADL, 2019).

but does not include other bias categories deemed by certain states to require statutory protection. Still, the variation in bias protected categories is only the first of two sources of misestimation of the prevalence of bias crimes.

Variation in Evidentiary Criteria

States also vary in the evidentiary standards required for prosecution of bias-motivated criminal conduct. Many states adopt the discriminatory selection model statutes. Considered to have the lowest threshold of culpability, the discriminatory selection model merely requires the "intentional selection" of a victim who is a member of a statutorily protected category. Thus, if an offender chooses a victim for criminal conduct because of his race, a hate crime charge could be supported under statutes that adopt the discriminatory selection model. Alternatively, if the offender chose the victim for criminal conduct because of their hair or eye color, a hate crime charge would not be supported under discriminatory selection statutes. Discriminatory selection statutes require both the discriminatory selection *and* the victim membership in a protected bias category. Critics of discriminatory selection statutes argue they cast too broad a net and can potentially include offenders whom discriminatorily select their victim without animus-related bias intent.

Under discriminatory selection statutes, animus against a particular statutorily protected group is not required for prosecution. In lieu of animus, discriminatory selection meets the threshold criteria for a bias crime arrest and prosecution. Undoubtedly, discriminatory selection statutes are administratively convenient for law enforcement because the threshold for establishing bias intent is merely the discriminatory selection of a protected class victim without regard to whether any type of group animus is apparent against the victim (Lawrence, 1999). For example, the Virginia and Wisconsin hate crime statutes were conceptualized as discriminatory selection statutes legislatively intended to require lightest prosecutorial burden, the "intentional selection" of a protected class victim. Accordingly, pursuant to Va. St. § 18:2–57 (2004), "A mandatory prison term is required if the person intentionally selects the person against whom (the crime is committed) because of his race, religion conviction, color, or national origin". Likewise, the Wisconsin (Wi. St. § 939.645, 1996) discriminatory selection hate crime statute provides that:

(1) If a person intentionally selects the person against whom the crime under par. (a) is committed or selects the property that is damaged or otherwise affected by the crime under par. (a) in whole or in part because of the actor's belief or perception regarding the race, religion, color, disability, sexual orientation, national origin or ancestry of that person or the owner or occupant of that property, whether or not the actor's belief or perception was correct.

The Wisconsin statute is of special note because the discriminatory selection clause of the statute was upheld after a challenge on First and Fourteenth Amendment

Equal Protection and Due Process grounds. Subsequent to the upholding of the Wisconsin statute, in *Wisconsin v. Mitchell* (1993), other states enacted similar discriminatory selection statutes based on Wisconsin's prototype model that withstood constitutional challenges.

Other states mandate much stronger evidence of animus-centered bias reflected in statutory language that requires evidence of maliciousness to support a hate crime charge. For instance, in the states of New Hampshire and Vermont, animus is demonstrated only when there is proof of malicious conduct toward statutorily protected classes of potential victims. However, legal scholars have found that proving malicious intent is a high prosecutorial burden to meet. Consequently, enforcement of hate crime statutes in these states are not as administratively convenient, and arguably less prevalent. Consider the animus-based New Hampshire (N.H. Rev. Stat. 651§If, 1995) statute as typical. To support a hate crime conviction, defendants must have been found to be "substantially motivated to commit the crime because of hostility towards the victim's religion, race, creed, sexual orientation, national origin, or sex" as defined in RSA § 21:49.

Similarly, the Vermont statute also requires proof of animus. According to 13 Vt. St. § 1455 (1990):

> A person who commits, causes to be committed, or attempts to commit any crime and whose conduct is maliciously motivated by the victim's actual or perceived race, color, religion, national origin, sex, ancestry, age, service in the U.S. Armed Forces, disability as defined by the VSA §. 485d (5), sexual orientation, or gender identity shall be subject to the following penalties.

Both sample typical animus statutes mandate a strict evidentiary requirement necessary to prove the state of mind of the offender. Both necessitate probable cause or proof that the bias conduct was "malicious motivated" by the victim's actual or perceived membership in a protected group. The problem with the statutory language of these statutes is that the perceived motive is quite subjective and largely determined by the offender's psyche. Morsch (1991) explained that the burden of proving racist motives is centered in the amorphous nature of motive itself. He posited "motive is the cause of one's actions whether one adopts the means to achieve those ends or consciously selects those ends" (Morsch, 1991, p. 666). Consequently, policing and prosecuting hate crimes is often dependent upon circumstantial evidence to infer bias-related motives. Morsch (1991) lamented the prosecutorial dilemma and impossibility of proving bias motives derived from circumstantial evidence all while trying to distinguishing them from all other possible motives. Given this enormous burden, it is quite understandable, why hate crime prosecutions may not be as prevalent in states that employ racial animus evidentiary criteria especially compared to those that employ discriminatory selection models (Lawrence, 1999).

Most states do not employ pure discriminatory selection or racial animus models and prefer slight variations of the two in the form of "because of "or "by reason of" statutes. States that have constructed these types of statutes look to their non-bias crime counterpart, and secondly the motivation reflected by the "because of" or "by reason of" the victim's membership in a protected group. Lawrence (1999) notes that in absence of the evidentiary requirement of animus in "because of" statutes, courts tend to interpret discriminatory selection as the central evidentiary requirement that also happens to typically be found in the civil rights anti-discrimination context. California's penalty enhancing bias crime statute (Cal Pen § 422.55, 2004) illustrates a typical example of the statutory construction of "because of" statutes:

> Hate Crime is a criminal act committed, in whole or in part, because of one or more of the following actual or perceived characteristics of the victim: Disability, Gender, Nationality, Race or Ethnicity, Religion, Sexual Orientation, and Association with person or group with one or more of these actual or perceived characteristics.

Additionally, the New York bias crime "because of" statute also leans toward the discriminatory selection model. Note the specific reference to the implications of "intentional selection" within the "because of" membership in a statutory protected group and the absence of a specific requirement of proof of animus or malice.

> A person commits a hate crime when he or she commits a specified offense and intentionally selects the person against whom the offense is committed or intended to be committed in whole or in substantial part because of a belief or perception regarding race, color, national origin, ancestry, gender, religion, religious practice, age, disability or sexual orientation of the person. (NY Pen § 485.05, 2000)

State statutes that incorporate the language "because of" and "proof of maliciousness" requirement in their statutes would appear to reflect a greater concern for the motivation of the offender. The term maliciousness asserts a requirement that the offender demonstrated a hatred for the victim (Lawrence, 1999). However, some courts still lean toward the discriminatory selection model in these statutes as well. In *Washington v. Talley* 22 Wn.2d 192 (1993), the Washington Supreme Court interpreted the "because of" and "maliciousness" language in their statute to mean discriminatory selection of the victim. The Court ruled that bigotry is a protected class of expression but disagreed that the Washington hate crime statute punished bigotry. Rather they asserted the statute punished the discriminatory act of selecting a victim based on his or her race status.

The evidentiary requirements to define and enforce hate crimes laws significantly varies from state to state and this undoubtedly has significant methodological limitations that adversely affect our ability to accurately estimate the prevalence of hate crimes (Pezzella, 2017). The absence of consensus on the proof criteria that constitutes a hate crime makes it almost impossible to measure how much hate crime there is in the United States. Unfortunately, the combination of variations in statutorily protected groups and each state's unique evidentiary criteria has significant ramifications on our capacity to accurately measure hate crime prevalence. Unless a broader more victim inclusive definition of hate crime is derived along with uniform evidentiary criteria, estimating the true prevalence of hates will likely be underreported.

Contemporary Hate Crime Jurisprudence

Criminal Causes of Action

Hate crime laws have largely evolved because of several landmark Supreme Court cases that have set the legal parameters for the statutory construction of contemporary hate crime laws. Hate crime laws are quite nuanced because of their proximity to protected expressions and behaviors under the First Amendment. Moreover, discriminatory selection and penalty enhancement provisions of hate crime statutes have been challenged on 14th Amendment Equal Protection and Due Process grounds.

One of the first cases to challenge the constitutionality of hate crime statutes was *RAV v. The City of St. Paul* (505 U.S. 377) 1992. The Court in *RAV* decided the first of several Supreme Court cases that examined the legality of state hate crime statutes. In *RAV*, the city of St Paul, Minnesota's bias ordinance was challenged on First and Fourteenth Amendment grounds. The case involved a skinhead offender who burnt a cross on the lawn of a black family's home with the intention to intimidate in violation of the St. Paul, Minnesota bias-motivated crime ordinance that prohibits the display of symbols which one knows or has reason to know "arouses anger, alarm or resentment in others on the basis of race, color, creed, religion or gender." The appellant challenged the statute as being overbroad and impermissibly content based. The Court accepted the Minnesota Supreme Court's narrow construction of the statute to only apply to "fighting words" that are unprotected by the First Amendment (*Chaplinsky v. New Hampshire*, 1942) and rejected the appellants over breadth claim. However, the Court also ruled the ordinance was impermissibly content inclusive. Specifically, the Court deemed the ordinance facially unconstitutional because it imposed special prohibitions on those speakers who express views on disfavored subjects of "race, color, creed, religion, or gender." Only those invectives that related to disfavored subjects were targeted by the ordinance. The Court reasoned that the ordinance reflected impermissible viewpoint discrimination.

The *RAV* decision was quite significant because it provided legal parameters for subsequent state and local legislation. Still, there was significant controversy regarding the Courts indecision on the defendant's over breadth claim. The decision in *RAV* had ramification for all state and localities that either enacted, or intended to enact, legislation that targeted specific bias types.

States did not have to wait long for clarity regarding the statutory construction and parameters of hate crime statutes. In 1993, the Court examined the constitutionality of another type of hate crime statute. In *Wisconsin v. Mitchell* (1993) the Court ruled on the state's penalty enhancement statute provision. A jury convicted Todd Mitchell, an African American defendant, of aggravated battery on a White victim after viewing a racially charged film, Mississippi Burning. Importantly, they found Mitchell intentionally selected his victim because of his race. Under the Wisconsin

intentional selection statute, an aggravated battery felony sentence is enhanced by 5
years when the defendant "intentionally selects" his victim "because of his race,
religion, color, disability, sexual orientation national origin, or ancestry of that person". The defendant appealed the Wisconsin statute asserting it was unconstitution-
ally vague and that the penalty enhancement provision punished his offensive
thoughts. The appellant also claimed the statute violated his rights to Equal
Protection under the Fourteenth Amendment.

The Court in *Wisconsin* found it paramount to distinguish the Wisconsin ordinance from the St. Paul, Minnesota ordinance previously found facially invalid in
RAV. Writing on behalf of the Court, Justice Rehnquist asserted: "The Wisconsin
law was aimed at punishing criminal conduct and a physical assault and is by no
stretch of the imagination expressive conduct protected by the First Amendment."
The Court also rejected the contention that the Wisconsin law would have chilling
effect on the future speech and expression. Finally, the Court posited that hate crime
laws much like anti-discrimination laws do not violate perpetrators free speech
rights because even in the presence of bias, absent the prohibited conduct there
would be no legal sanction. The Court's decision in *Wisconsin* provided the statutory framework for subsequent hate crime legislation throughout the country. States
that sought to employ pure or some version of the evidentiary criteria of "intentional
selection" could now rely on the *Wisconsin* precedent to enhance sentences for bias
motivated conduct against statutorily protected bias categories. Moreover, the court
ruled that penalty enhancement statutes for bias crimes was a valid and constitutional sentencing option.

The constitutionality of penalty enhancement statutes again came under scrutiny
in *Apprendi v. New Jersey* 530 U.S. 466. (2000). In *Apprendi*, the appellant was
allegedly committed a racially motivated crime wherein he fired several .22 caliber
bullets into the home of an African American family that had recently moved into
the neighborhood. Apprendi took a plea to gun possession but denied the racial bias
motivation and asserted the attack was a result of intoxication. The trial judge found
"by a preponderance of the evidence" that Apprendi's crime was motivated by racial
bias and sentenced him to 12 years, a 2-year sentencing enhancement above the
maximum for a non-bias related weapons charge. Apprendi appealed and both the
New Jersey Superior and Supreme Courts affirmed the sentencing enhancement
holding it was a sentencing factor in lieu of an element of the crime and therefore
not subject to the jury trial and proof by a reasonable doubt constitutional
requirement.

The United States Supreme Court decided otherwise. They held that the Sixth
Amendment right to a jury trial incorporated to the states through the Fourteenth
Amendment prohibited judges from enhancing criminal sentences beyond the statutory maximum based on facts other than those decided by a jury beyond a reasonable doubt.

The decisions in *RAV*, *Mitchell*, and *Apprendi* have shaped hate crime jurisprudence and statutory construction of hate crime laws particularly in terms of the
constitutionality of intentional selection and penalty enhancement provisions.

However, federal and state laws also provide additional sanctions in the form of civil actions against hate crime offenders convicted of bias related crimes.

Civil Causes of Action

Recall 45 states and the District of Columbia have enacted hate crime statutes for offenders who commit bias-motivated crimes. A total of 32 of these states have also provided civil causes of actions for defendants convicted of bias crimes. Bias motivated civil causes of action statutes are quite similar to their criminal cause of action counterparts in some important ways. Both limit their cause of action for bias injuries to statutorily protected bias categories. Moreover, in civil bias matters, the "intentional selection" proof criteria are applied to the relatively lighter evidentiary standard the "preponderance of the evidence." In many states, the terms of the civil action law suits are not dependent on whether a criminal cause of action was brought or for that matter successful. Typically, state civil actions for bias-motivated injuries provides petitioners with a range of reliefs including injunctions, actual and punitive damages for economic and non-economic loss including damages for emotional distress, and reasonable attorney and expert witness. A close examination of the civil action statutes for the District of Columbia (D.C. Code §22-3704, 1990), and the states of Nevada (NRS §41.690, 2015), New York (NY CLS Civ R §79n, 2010), and Oregon (ORS §30-198, 2019) illustrate typical civil action remedies for the 32 states that have enacted civil causes of actions for both criminal and non-criminal bias related injuries. All four of these statutes provide for relief in the form of such as injunctions, actual, nominal, general, punitive and special damages for emotional distress, and sometimes attorney fees and costs. In the D.C. and Oregon statutes, parents of minors who cause bias motivated injuries to person and or property are liable for damages. Also, the New York and D.C. statutes incorporate the specific language of "intentional selection" as the proof criteria.

With respect to measuring the prevalence of civil remedied bias crimes, civil actions suffer from the same problems of criminal actions that obfuscate understanding the scope of bias crimes in the United States. Those that require intentional selection cast such a wide net that respondents who were not necessarily bias motivated may find themselves liable when bias was not really the driving force behind the alleged injury. In addition, only statutorily protected bias categories have the standing to proceed with a bias motivated civil action. Similarly, states with civil actions that require a more stringent criteria than intentional selection, such as the Nevada statute may find proving bias motivation difficult even with the lighter preponderance of the evidence standard. The Nevada statute requires evidence of willful violation of a perpetrator who was motivated by the injured person characteristics. Like criminal causes of actions, proving willfulness and motivation may be a difficult burden to overcome even by respondents in civil action law suits.

Importance of Accurate Measurement

We know from American history that hate crimes are a pervasive form of offending that is geographically dispersed throughout the United States. The review of the legislative history of hate crimes clearly indicate the stability and prevalence of hate crimes. Contemporary hate crimes statutes constructed to proscribe hate crimes have also been shaped significantly by the decisions in *RAV*, *Mitchell*, and *Apprendi*. Undoubtedly, these decisions also influence whether hate crime charges are sought by police and prosecutors and consequently have a bearing on the classifications of hate crimes.

Despite the legislative and judicial history of hate crimes throughout the contemporary hate crime era, efforts to measure the prevalence of hate crimes has been less than accurate (Comey, 2014). Only recently have we attempted to develop some measures to assess the prevalence of hate crimes. The HCSA of 1990 was the first legislation to authorize the annual collection of hate crime data on a voluntary basis from participating police agencies. However, the annual UCR Hate Crime Statistics report has been roundly criticized as an inaccurate estimate of hate crime data for several reasons. First, the UCR only reports hate crimes known to police and does not reflect or reference the dark figure of unreported hate crimes (Pezzella et al., 2019). Secondly, due to the voluntary nature of police participation, only 75% of police agencies nationally participate in the program. Of those, on average 80% have reported zero hate crimes since the beginning of the data collection efforts in 1990 (USCCR, 2019). As a consequence of these various defects in collections, the UCR hate crime reporting program produces counts that woefully underreport the occurrence and severity of hate crimes.

Still, using UCR estimates as a baseline, recent reports indicate that hate crimes are soaring at record levels. UCR hate crime reports over the 3-year period of 2015–2017 indicate that hate crimes spiked in consecutive years. Moreover, Levin and Grisham (2017) found even larger patterned increases in the nations ten largest cities. In 2018, ethnic, primarily anti-Hispanic bias, demonstrated the largest proportional growth. These patterns are important to note but caution is advised because of the limitations of UCR data that substantially underreport hate crimes. These limitations are very apparent in the light of victimization studies that have found a significant dark figure of hate crime underreporting (Pezzella et al., 2019).

Although UCR incident and BJS victimization reports reflect different measures of prevalence, the magnitude of the differences is alarming. Still, the BJS special reports suggest a lot more variation in the most prevalent victimization categories than the bias categories depicted in the UCR hate crime reports. These alternating explanations of the occurrence and severity of hate crimes presents an important policy enigma. Contemporary hate crime statutes reflect consensus and policy choices concerning the bias categories each state and the federal government statutorily chooses to provide special protection. Offenders who commit a bias-motivated criminal act against a member of a protected bias victim category are subject to an enhanced penalty. It is vitally important to accurately measure hate crimes because understanding occurrences by bias categories and types inform policymakers. Ideally, policymakers can incorporate group-based prevalence and the severity of hate crimes in legislation that focuses treatment modalities on groups and individuals likely to be victimized. A refocus of our attention to measurement accuracy is a prerequisite to providing protection and treatment to victims that normally will not report hate crime incidents or injuries to law enforcement. Only then can we assert that our evidence-based hate crime policy coincides with victim needs.

References

Anti-Defamation League. (2012). *Hate crime laws*. http://www.adl.org/sites/default/files/documents/assets/pdf/combating-hate/Hate-Crime-.pdf
Anti-Defamation League. (2019). *Anti-defamation league state hate crime statutory provisions*. http://www.adl.org/
Apprendi v. New Jersey. (2000). U.S. Supreme Court (530 U.S. 466).
Ca. Pen § 422.55 (2004).
Chakraborti, N., & Garland, J. (2012). Reconceptualizing hate crime victimization through the lens of vulnerability and "difference". *Theoretical Criminology, 16*(4), 499–514.
Chaplinski v. New Hampshire. (1942). U.S. Supreme Court (315 U.S. 568).
Comey, J. (2014). *The FBI and the ADL: Working toward a world without hate*. Retrieved from https://www.fbi.gov/news/speeches/the-fbi-and-the-adl-working-toward-a-world-without-hate
D.C. Code § 22-3704 (1990).
Grattet, R., & Jenness, V. (2001). The birth and maturation of hate crime policy in the United States. *American Behavioral Scientist, 45*(4), 668–696.
Jacobs, J. B., & Potter, K. (1998). *Hate crimes: Criminal law & identity politics*. New York: Oxford University Press.
Jenness, V., & Broad, K. (1997). *Hate crimes: New social movements and the politics of violence*. New Brunswick, NJ: Transaction Publishers.
Lawrence, F. M. (1999). *Punishing hate: Bias crimes under American law*. Cambridge, MA: Harvard University Press.
Levin, B. (2002). From slavery to hate crime laws: The emergence of race and status-based protection in American criminal law. *Journal of Social Issues, 58*(2), 227–245.
Levin, B. H., & Grisham, K. (2017). *Hate crimes rise in major American localities in 2016* (p. 29). Washington, DC: United States Department of Justice Hate Crime Summit.
Mallett, R. K., Huntsinger, J. R., & Swim, J. K. (2011). The role of system-justification motivation, group status and system threat in directing support for hate crimes legislation. *Journal of Experimental Social Psychology, 47*(2), 384–390.
Masucci, M., & Langton, L. (2017). *Hate crime victimization, 2004–2015*. Washington, DC: US Department of Justice Office of Justice Programs, Bureau of Justice Statistics.
McDevitt, J., Levin, J., & Bennett, S. (2002). Hate crime offenders: An expanded typology. *Journal of Social Issues, 58*(2), 303–317.
Morsch, J. (1991). The problem of motive in hate crimes: The argument against presumptions of racial motivation. *Journal of Criminal Law and Criminology, 82*, 659.
N.H. Rev. Stat. § 651.6. (1995).
NRS § 41.690. (2015).
NY CLS Civ R § 79n. (2010).
NY Pen § 485.05. (2000).
ORS. § 30-198. (2019).

Pezzella, F. S. (2017). *Hate crime statutes: A public policy and law enforcement dilemma*. Cham: Springer.

Pezzella, F. S., Fetzer, M. D., & Keller, T. (2019). The dark figure of hate crime underreporting. *American Behavioral Scientist*, 0002764218823844. https://doi.org/10.1177/0002764218823844

RAV v. City of St Paul, Minnesota. (1992). U.S. Supreme Court (505 U.S. 377).

Title 18 U.S.C. § 247, Damage to Religious Property Pub. L. No. 104–155. (1996).

Title 18 U.S.C. § 249, Matthew Shepard and James Byrd Jr., Hate Crime Prevention Act of 2009 Ch. 13 Pub. L. 111-84. (2009).

Title 18 U.S.C. § 1994, The Hate Crime Sentencing Enhancement Act of 1994.

Title 28 U.S.C. § 994, Hate Crime Statistics Act of 1990, Pub. L. No. 101–275, 28. (1990).

Title 42 U.S.C. § 13701, Violence Against Women Act., Public Health and Welfare (1994).

United States Commission on Civil Rights. (2019). In the name of hate (Publication No. 11–13). Retrieved from https://www.usccr.gov/pubs/2019/11-13-in-the-name-of-hate.pdf

Va. St. §18 2–57. (2004).

Vt. St. 13 §1455. (1990).

Washington v. Talley. (1993). 22 Wn.2d 192.

Wi. St. §939.645. (1996).

Wisconsin v. Mitchell. (1993). U.S. Supreme Court (505 U.S. 476).

Chapter 2
The Conceptualization of Hate Crime

Abstract This chapter focuses on how hate crime is conceptualized in America. Hate crime is deconstructed into two components – bias motivation and criminal offenses – and discussion is provided for how each component is conceptualized. We begin by explaining what bias motivation entails and how it is legally defined. Bias motivation categories are distinguished from bias types, and definitions are provided for the bias motivation categories recognized by the Hate Crime Statistics Act (1990). The conceptualization of bias motivation relevant to perception and association is addressed along with the idea of intersectionality or multiple bias. Regarding the crime component of hate crimes, we clarify the difference between bias incidents and hate crime. Examples of how criminal behaviors are defined as hate crimes are provided, and offenses common to hate crime identified and described. We discuss how there can be different victim types depending upon the type of hate crime committed. The chapter is concluded by showing how hate crime can be cross-classified or misclassified with other types of criminal behaviors. The topics covered in this chapter are designed to provide foundational knowledge for the conceptualization of hate crime and how this translates to its measurement.

Keywords Bias categories · Bias crime · Bias motivation · Bias types · Criminal offense · Cross-classification · Hate crime · Intersectionality · Perceived bias · Victim type

To begin studying hate crime in the United States, one must first have a working definition of this concept and then understand how hate crimes are measured in this country. This is no easy task, as hate crime is a class of criminal behavior with lots of complexities. It is important to understand these complexities in order to adequately measure hate crime. This chapter is designed to address the conceptualization of hate crime, while Chap. 3 will focus more on its operationalization. The current chapter provides some background on how hate crime has been defined in the literature. The term, hate crime, is deconstructed in order to show what components are required for such an event to occur. Each component is then explored in depth, so that the reader will have a better understanding of what a hate crime is conceptually and how this will translate into its measurement.

First, it is warranted to explain that the term "bias crime" is sometimes used as an alternative for hate crime in the literature. Hate crime and bias crime can be used interchangeably as conceptually they refer the same phenomenon. The term itself, hate crime, can be misleading as it would infer that it is a crime perpetrated out of hate, and this is not always the case. The more adequate and precise term would be that of bias crime, however, hate crime has become the more accepted and widely used vernacular for such criminal behavior.

Sample Definitions

When studying hate crimes, whether for an academic class, research, policy development or whatever the case may be, it becomes evident that there is no single, universal definition for this concept. Some definitions are simple and concise while others are much more detailed and complex. By looking across these definitions and comparing them, there are some standard elements that become evident as to what a hate crime involves. A simple definition for a hate crime or bias crime is "a crime committed as an act of prejudice" (Lawrence, 1999, p. 9). Phyllis Gerstenfeld offers her definitional variation as "a criminal act that is motivated, at least in part, by the group affiliation of the victim" (2018, p. 5). Both definitions recognize that a crime or a criminal act must be involved in the incident. Both also recognize that there must be some element of hate or bias, in that the offense was committed as a result of prejudice or directed towards the victim's group affiliation. These two examples provide conceptual definitions that are simple and brief, but there is still some ambiguity as to what is meant by group affiliation.

When definitions are provided for legal or measurement purposes, they become more precise and begin to address this idea of group affiliation. For instance, the Federal Bureau of Investigation (FBI) defines a hate crime as "a criminal offense against a person or property motivated in whole or in part by an offender's bias against a race, religion, disability, sexual orientation, ethnicity, gender, or gender identity" (FBI, n.d.). The FBI's definition expounds on the offense type as well as specifies categories of bias motivation. These categories of bias motivation refer to a victim's group affiliation. A racially motivated hate crime, for example, might involve a targeted victim because that person was African American. Here the victim's group affiliation or membership would be being identified with persons of the African American race. A similar definition of hate crimes comes from the current Hate Crime Statistics Act (HCSA). Here, hate crimes are defined as "crimes that manifest evidence of prejudice based on race, gender and gender identity, religion, disability, sexual orientation, or ethnicity, including where appropriate the crimes of murder, non-negligent manslaughter; forcible rape; aggravated assault, simple assault, intimidation; arson; and destruction, damage or vandalism of property"

(Hate Crime Statistics Act, 1990). This definition identifies seven bias motivation categories and eight criminal offenses that are recognized as hate crimes in this country. The increased level of detail in the HCSA's and FBI's definitions aids with identifying and tracking hate crimes.

Regardless of the level of detail provided by definitions of hate crime, there are two common themes that can be identified. There is an evident bias component for the motivation of the offense and there is the offense itself. The bias reflects prejudice towards the victim based upon certain characteristics or group membership, and the criminal offense is motivated by said bias.

The Deconstruction of "Hate Crime"

At a fundamental level, a hate crime is comprised of two essential components that must coincide with one another to qualify as a hate crime. The first component, the hate, is that the offender's actions must have been motivated by bias. The second component is that the offender's actions must be a criminal offense. That is, the behavior that was perpetrated must be defined by statute as a criminal act. Either component by itself is insufficient to qualify as a hate crime. In order for a hate crime to occur, both components need to occur simultaneously in the same incident. To better understand what the concept of hate crime involves, each of these components are explored in depth next.

The Hate Component

In conceptualizing hate crime, several aspects referring to the "hate" component need to be addressed. To begin, some basic terminology is presented including what bias motivation is. This leads into a discussion of how bias motivation is legally defined. Distinctions are then made between bias motivation categories and bias types. The bias motivation categories recognized by the Hate Crime Statistics Act are identified and defined. This section on the hate component of hate crimes concludes with an explanation of perception and association, followed by content about multiple bias and intersectionality.

There have been many terms used to exemplify the hate component of hate crime. This part of a hate crime may be indicated by alternative phrases such as bias, prejudice, antipathy, or animus and reflect the offender's hostility towards the victim because of some characteristic or trait that identifies group affiliation. There is also the underlying element of discriminatory selection or targeting of the victim because that victim exhibits characteristics of or is affiliated with a particular group which the offender has hatred or hostility towards. Some definitions of hate crime may stipulate bias by simply using the phrase "group affiliation," while others may use phrases such as "race," "religion," or "sexual orientation" to address why the victim was targeted. Essentially, this establishes the motivation for the offense occurring, and arguably sets hate crimes apart from ordinary crimes. Hate crimes only occur because this bias or prejudice exists, and without it, the offense would not occur. Furthermore, the victim is not targeted specifically because of who they are as an individual, but because they exhibit a characteristic that identifies them will a larger group. Lawrence (1999) addresses this with his discussion of victim interchangeability, in which any victim would be sufficient so long as that person shares the characteristic. That is enough to motivate the offender's behavior.

Bias Is Required, Not Hate

The motivation for this type of criminal behavior needs to be addressed. The concept, hate crime, would seem to indicate that the offender truly has hatred towards the victim's group. This can sometimes be a source of confusion when studying hate crime because what actually qualifies as "hate." Furthermore, some offenses may actually be perpetrated out of hate, but not qualify as a hate crime. For example, an individual may victimize their ex-spouse out of anger and hatred towards the victim, but conceptually this would not be a hate crime. A hate crime occurs not because of *who* the victim is but instead *what* the victim is (Lawrence, 1999). The offender's bias is directed towards what the victim is – a member of the group.

It may very well be the case that the offender is motivated by hatred, but realistically, true hatred is not the threshold that must be met for hate crimes. The actual degree of hostility required is that of prejudice or bias. This prejudice or bias is not towards just the victim but to all members of that group, such as all members of that victim's race or all members of that victim's gender. It is important to recognize and distinguish that the criminal act is motivated by bias and not necessarily by hate, despite the fact that the conceptual term seems to indicate that hate is a requirement. This is why the phrase "bias crime" would be a more accurate and appropriate label than "hate crime" for these phenomena, as bias crime is conceptually more intuitive. Either phrase can be used, but the latter phrase is utilized more often.

An additional note on the motivation of hate crimes is that bias does not need to be the sole motivator for the crime occurring. The FBI's definition for hate crime illustrates this by utilizing the phrasing "motivated in whole or in part by an offender's bias" (n.d.). An offense will still be a hate crime so long as it is at least partially motivated by bias. This recognizes that some hate crimes might have additional motivations including the offender's bias. Scholars have identified some of these additional motivations as committing hate crimes for the thrill or excitement factor, in defense of one's turf, in retaliation to a previous hate crime, and as a mission to eliminate certain groups (Levin & McDevitt, 1993; McDevitt, Levin, & Bennett, 2002). While these four examples are not an exhaustive list of all the other motivations for hate crimes, they do provide context as to how hate crimes may be motivated by more than just the offender's bias.

Bias Motivations Legally Defined

Much as the crime aspect of a hate crime must be legally defined, the hate component must also be legally defined. This means that legal statute must specify which groups are recognized as "protected" by law if a member of the group is targeted. Herein lies a significant issue in the conceptualization of hate crime. There is significant variation across the country as to which groups are protected and which groups are not. Legal statutes defining these protected groups exist at both the federal and state levels. There may be congruence or disparities across these federal and state statutes as to which groups are legally recognized as protected (ADL, 2019; Gerstenfeld, 1992; Petrosino, 1999). Unfortunately, there is more disparity than congruence across statutes. The lack of consensus about who should be protected by hate crime legislation convolutes its conceptualization and accurate measurement.

Bias Motivation Category Versus Bias Type

Distinctions need to be made between the terms "bias motivation category" and "bias type" when conceptualizing hate crimes. Bias motivations categories are a broader or more general method of classifying bias, while bias types are more specific. It might help to view bias motivation categories as a variable and bias types as the attributes for that variable. Bias motivation categories would be race, ethnicity, religion, sexual orientation, disability, gender, or gender identity, and these reflect general areas of bias motivation. Bias types are the specific groups within these broad bias motivation classifications. The bias motivation category of gender includes bias types for males and females. So, if a hate crime was perpetrated against a victim because the offender is biased against females, gender would be the bias motivation category and the bias type would be female bias or anti-female. A hate crime perpetrated because the offender has bias against African Americans would have a bias motivation category of race and a bias type of anti-African American. Bias motivation categories are a more general classification of the offender's bias, whereas bias type is more specific and allows for the targeted group to be identified. This is important to understand in the conceptualization of hate crime, and it becomes even more important when measuring hate crimes. Bias motivation categories and types are also important to understand when looking at hate crime laws.

Hate crime laws, typically, do not specify protected groups in writing or statutory language. Instead, traditionally what has been done is that a broader classification is articulated in statutes that will include protected groups under it. In looking back at the HCSA's (1990) definition, "crimes that manifest evidence of prejudice based on race, gender and gender identity, religion, disability, sexual orientation, or ethnicity…," one can see how these broader classifications or bias motivation categories are used. For example, race is utilized in the statutory language and this broad classification includes African Americans, a group that has been historically targeted for hate crimes. By using race in the statute, this then includes all racial groups, not just African Americans. This is noteworthy because one argument against hate crime legislation is that it gives greater protection to certain groups and not others. Such an argument becomes moot because the inclusion and protection of all racial groups is an application of the Equal Protection Clause for the First and Fourteenth Amendments of the U.S. Constitution. However, in cases where state hate crime laws actually specify groups such as "law enforcement officers" (e.g., Louisiana Revised Statutes 14 § 170.2, 2016), a particular occupation is being protected and not all occupations. When this happens, the argument that certain groups are given greater protection could be made.

Because this book is devoted to the measurement of hate crimes in the entire United States, the classifications included in the HCSA can be viewed as the standard for which groups are recognized as protected. Currently, at the national level, all groups are protected within the seven bias motivation categories of race, ethnicity, religion, sexual orientation, disability, gender, and gender identity. There has been an evolution over time as to which groups are legally defined as protected. At its conception in 1990, groups based on race, ethnicity, religion, and sexual orientation were recognized under the Hate Crime Statistics Act. Disabled persons were recognized in 1994, followed by groups targeted because of their gender or gender identity which were added in 2009 (HCSA, 1990). It is significant to understand that this means the "hate" component of hate crimes has changed conceptually over time with the inclusion of these additional categories. Furthermore, it should be recognized that the conceptual definition of hate crime may very well change in the future if additional categories of bias motivation are added.

Definitions of Bias Motivation Categories

To fully comprehend how hate crime is conceptualized, the various bias motivations need to be defined. In terms of definitions for bias motivation categories as well as bias motivation types, the best source currently comes from the FBI's "Hate Crime Data Collection Guidelines and Training Manual" (2015). Definitions for the broader bias motivation categories of race, ethnicity, religion, sexual orientation, disability, gender, and gender identity are as follows:

Racial bias focuses on persons "who possess common physical characteristics, e.g., color of skin, eyes, and/or hair, facial features, etc., genetically transmitted by descent and heredity which distinguish them as a distinct division of humankind, e.g., Asians, Blacks or African Americans, Whites" (p. 11). This category is a classic example of immutable characteristics that are unchangeable as they are biological characteristics that are acquired at birth. Ethnic bias is closely related to racial bias with the difference being that ethnicity is focused more on culture than biology. This is bias against those "whose members identify with each other, through a common heritage, often consisting of a common language, common culture and/or ideology that stresses common ancestry" (p. 11). Religious bias directs hostility towards individuals "who share the same religious beliefs regarding the origin and purpose of the universe and the existence or nonexistence of a supreme being" (p. 13). Within this category of bias motivation, bias would be recognized against commonly targeted religious groups such as members of the Jewish faith. This category also includes additional religions as well as atheism. Sexual orientation bias focuses on a "a person's physical, romantic, and/or emotional attraction to members of the same and/or opposite sex" (p. 15). Here, sexual orientation includes persons who are heterosexual, bisexual, and homosexual, but not transgendered persons. Bias based upon disability refers to an individual's "physical or mental impairments, whether such disability is temporary or permanent, congenital or acquired by heredity, accident, injury, advanced age, or illness" (p. 9). The two most recent additions to the HCSA include gender and gender identity bias. Gender bias relates to one's biological sex at birth (FBI, 2015). Gender identity bias reflects antipathy towards a "person's internal sense of being male, female, or a combination of both" (p. 10). One's gender identity may not be identical with one's gender. Gender identity includes transgendered persons. The FBI's definitions are quite helpful for understanding what the current bias motivation categories of the HCSA represent.

Be aware that these definitions are specific to the FBI and may not be exactly the same for other agencies or jurisdictions. California, for example, recognizes gender as a bias motivation category in its hate crime legislation, but gender is defined in such a way that it includes both gender (i.e., a person's biological sex) and gender identity (i.e., a person's gender expression) (California Penal Code § 422.56, 2019). Here gender identity is absorbed by the category of gender as the two are closely related. Awareness of differences in definitions is paramount when conceptualizing and accurately measuring hate crime.

Perception and Association

Additional complexities to understanding hate crimes involve the elements of perception and association. Here, perception refers to the offender's mistaken perceptions of the victim, and association refers to the victim essentially being a bystander of the offender's bias. Both of these occur when the victim is not a member of the targeted group reflective of the offender's bias. Also note that both are still conceptualized as hate crime.

Looking first at perception, "even if the offender was mistaken about the victim's race, religion, disability, sexual orientation, ethnicity, gender, or gender identity, the offense is still a hate crime as long as the offender was motivated, in whole or in part, by bias against that group" (FBI, 2015, p. 7). An illustration would be if a victim who is Sikh had been targeted because the offender has bias against Muslims and mistook the victim for a Muslim. Even though the offender was incorrect about the victim's religion, the offense would still be classified as a hate crime. Furthermore, the bias type should reflect that of the offender's perceived bias despite the fact of mistaken perception. In the example above, the bias type would be anti-Muslim and not anti-Sikh. Thus, an offense will be a hate crime if the offender was at least partially motivated by bias, regardless of inaccurate perceptions.

Association is another element to be conceptually understood when studying hate crimes. It is possible to have a hate crime when the victim is not actually a member of a targeted group, but instead is somehow associated with said group. Here the victim is a bystander of the offender's bias but a direct target of the offense. Examples of hate crimes that pertain to association would include the victim being in a multi-racial couple but not from the targeted racial group or belonging to an advocacy group supporting the targeted group (FBI, 2015; Oudekerk, 2019). In either example, the victim is associated with a member or members of a group and was targeted because of the offender's bias against that group.

Multiple Bias

One last point of discussion on the bias component of hate crimes, is the real possibility that an incident may be perpetrated out of more than one bias. This is the notion that a hate crime incident may involve *multiple bias* or have *intersectionality*. Intersectionality is used here to refer to the multiple dimensions of one's identity (APA, 2017). As one's identity may be defined by multiple characteristics across race, ethnicity, religion, sexual orientation, gender, and gender identity, it is conceivable that a person may be targeted because of multiple characteristics and not just one. Hence, hate crime can be intersectional and involve more than one bias motivation.

Multiple bias in hate crime can exist in various ways and in many different possible combinations. Two general ways that multiple bias can arise are offered here with examples for each. First, multiple bias may exist across more than one bias motivation category. The targeted victim of a hate crime might have been chosen because that person exhibits characteristics that would classify them into more than one protected group and the offender has prejudice against these groups. Here an example might be due to the victim's sexual orientation and gender identity. A second way multiple bias might occur is when there are multiple victims with different characteristics that would classify them into different protected groups and the offender has prejudice against these groups. An example of this could be in the same bias motivation category, such as sexual orientation, but different bias types, such as one victim was a gay male and the other a lesbian female. Again, these are just a few examples to provide context, and there are numerous possibilities in which multiple bias might be present in hate crime.

The Crime Component

This portion of this chapter on the conceptualization of hate crimes focuses on understanding the crime component of hate crimes. First, discussion addresses bias incidents, which are related to hate crimes, but they are not hate crimes. Next, how hate crimes are legally defined with respect to the criminal offense aspect is presented. Following this, common offenses involved in hate crimes identified and described. The idea of the victim is then explored, followed by a review of how hate crime can overlap with other types of crime and may be misclassified.

Bias Incidents and Hate Speech

Some confusion may revolve around the "crime" component of hate crime, such that sometimes non-criminal behaviors get mistaken for hate crimes. One of the first points for clarification is that a hate crime, *must* involve a criminal offense. This means that the action that has been committed needs to be legally defined as a crime. Often, non-criminal acts that involve bias or prejudice may get confused as a hate crime, but such an act would only be a "bias incident." A bias incident and a hate crime are not one and the same. This is a very important distinction to be made. The SPLC (2017) clearly makes this distinction by explaining that hate crimes are unlawful acts motivated by bias versus bias incidents which are defined as "eruptions of hate where no crime is committed" (p. 1).

A typical example of a bias incident is one that involves hate speech. Hate speech is not a crime and is protected by the First Amendment of the U.S. Constitution. Hateful speech may very well "be intended to degrade, intimidate or incite violence or discrimination against certain groups" (Shanmugasundaram, 2018), but by itself, it does not constitute a hate crime. However, hate speech can be used as an indicator for substantiating the bias component of a hate crime, so long as a criminal offense was committed in the same incident. If an incident involved hate speech without the commission of a criminal offense, then this would be deemed a bias incident.

This book focuses on hate crimes not bias incidents. This is not done to downplay the significance or importance of bias incidents, as bias incidents occur in much greater frequency than hate crimes, have negative effects on those that the incidents are directed towards, and can be the precursors to or even escalate into hate crimes (SPLC, 2017).

Crimes Legally Defined

No single criminal offense typifies hate crime, but instead there are multiple types of crimes and offenses that could be classified as hate crime. So, what crimes can be hate crimes? A simple answer to this question would be any criminal offense, provided it is accompanied by a legally defined bias motivation. While there is truth in this answer, it is a bit simplistic and might be misconstrued to imply that any criminal offense could be a hate crime. This is not the case. With hate crime, the offense must directly affect another individual or entity – a victim per se. A victim is necessary for the bias motivation component of hate crimes, so offenses lacking a victim would not be able to qualify. Offenses that can qualify as hate crime need to be legally defined.

Criminal offenses are legally defined in criminal code at the federal and state levels. Every state defines which behaviors are criminal through statutory law, which is often referred to as criminal code or penal code. State criminal codes will specify all criminal offenses for that jurisdiction, but not every criminal offense can qualify as hate crime. Which criminal offenses qualify as hate crimes will also need to be stipulated in the criminal code. Prior discussion addressed how the bias component of hate crime are legally defined, now discussion turns to how this is done for the crime component.

There are several ways that a state can legally define a criminal offense as a hate crime. The most common method is through criminal code that elevates sanctions for hate crimes. This method will have a statutory code that legally defines hate crimes by outlining the bias motivation component and then lists or links specified offenses, also from statutory code, that would qualify as a hate crime. New York State for example, legally defines the bias component based on "race, color, national origin, ancestry, gender, religion, religious practice, age, disability, or sexual orientation," and lists all specified offenses that can be hate crimes such as "assault in the third degree … menacing in the first degree … murder in the second degree…" (New York Hate Crimes Act, 2000). New York legally defines both the bias motivations and specified offenses that are hate crimes in that jurisdiction.

Another method for legally defining hate crime is by codifying a specific behavior as a hate crime offense. New York also utilizes this method with its penal law for the offense of aggravated harassment in the first degree, which reads:

> A person is guilty of aggravated harassment in the first degree when with intent to harass, annoy, threaten or alarm another person, because of a belief or perception regarding such person's race, color, national origin, ancestry, gender, gender identity or expression, religion, religious practice, age, disability or sexual orientation, regardless of whether the belief or perception is correct, he or she … etches, paints, draws upon or otherwise places a swastika … sets on fire a cross in public view … etches, paints, draws upon or otherwise places or displays a noose…. (NYS Penal Law § 240.31, n.d.)

States may legally define specific offenses as hate crimes through the language in the actual definition of the offense. In the example above, the language used to define aggravated harassment in the first degree specifies bias motivation categories and identifies actions – displaying a swastika or noose or burning a cross – which are well established symbols of hate.

One last method is very similar to that of penalty enhancement statutes. Here bias motivation is legally defined and then legally defined criminal offenses are linked, but the difference is that the statute is for an "add-on" offense. Pennsylvania utilizes this method with the crime of ethnic intimidation which legally defines bias motivation as "malicious intention toward the race, color, religion or national origin of another individual or group of individuals" and commits a specified offense (18 Pa.C.S. § 2710, 2008). The crime of ethnic intimidation is a separate crime which cannot stand on its own and must accompany a traditional criminal offense. It is "added on" to increase punishment for offenders by having an additional criminal charge.

In summary, the crime aspect of hate crimes must also be legally defined. This is done through criminal codes which are statutes for criminal laws in a jurisdiction. Three methods were identified as to how this is done (1) through enhancement-type statutes which defines what bias motivations are recognized in a jurisdiction and then links specified offenses that can be hate crimes, (2) through creating offenses that, themselves, are legally defined as hate crimes, and (3) through an add-on type of criminal offense. These methods vary across states with hate crime laws, as do the terminology or labels used for offenses.

Recognizing the variation in how states legally define hate crime has direct relevance on the conceptualization of hate crime. To know and understand the nuances of each jurisdiction's criminal codes related to hate crime is an overwhelming task. Fortunately, these criminal codes can be transformed and combined into more general conceptual labels for crimes by using a statute cross-reference table, and this is the process that's followed when hate crime data are collected for measurement purposes. For instance, the New York State penal law for aggravated harassment in the first degree from the above example would be classified into a more general label of destruction, damage or vandalism or property (DCJS, 2019). These more general labels for crimes reflect those articulated in the Hate Crime Statistics Act and measured by the FBI.

Recall that at the federal level, hate crimes are defined in such a way that both bias motivations and crimes are specified. Again, the HCSA (1990) defines hate crimes as "crimes that manifest evidence of prejudice based on race, gender and gender identity, religion, disability, sexual orientation, or ethnicity, including where appropriate the crimes of murder, non-negligent manslaughter; forcible rape; aggravated assault, simple assault, intimidation; arson; and destruction, damage or vandalism of property." This definition identifies eight specific criminal offenses that are recognized as hate crimes for which data, at the very least, should be collected. Realize that these are not the only criminal offenses that can be hate crimes, but they are offenses that are recognized as important. As such, an understanding of what these offenses entail is necessary.

Common Offenses

Through the Hate Crime Statistics Act, Congress required the Attorney General to collect data on hate crimes, who in turn, delegated this task to the FBI (2019a). The FBI defines and measures the offenses of murder and non-negligent manslaughter, rape, aggravated assault, simple assault, intimidation, arson, and destruction, damage or vandalism of property as hate crimes. In looking at these offenses, it is evident that hate crime involves a diversity of crimes that range in level of harm, vary by type, and differ in who or what is targeted. Murder and non-negligent manslaughter, rape, aggravated assault, simple assault, and intimidation are crimes of violence that will have at least one individual as a victim. Since each of these offenses targets individuals as victims, they are categorized as crimes against persons. These criminal offenses cover a spectrum of severity of harm with intimidations involving threats but no physical attack to murder and non-negligent manslaughter that result in the death of the victim. Arson and destruction, damage or vandalism, on the other hand, are non-violent offenses involving no physical harm to a victim. They represent crimes against property which may not have an individual as a victim. If there is not an individual victim, then who or what is the victim in these types of hate crimes? This leads to an important discussion about hate crimes and the idea of the victim.

The Idea of the Victim

Up until this point, discussion of how hate crime is defined has inferred that there is a victim who was targeted because of their group affiliation and the offender's bias towards that group. This idea of a victim implies that there is an individual or person whom the crime was committed against. While individual persons are often victims of hate crimes, there can be other entities that are the targets of bias-motivated offenses. This is acknowledged in the FBI's definition of hate crime, which is "a criminal offense against a person or property motivated in whole or in part by an offender's bias against a race, religion, disability, sexual orientation, ethnicity, gender, or gender identity" (FBI, n.d.). The FBI's definition differentiates between crimes against persons and crimes against property, and in doing so this expands the idea of the victim or what is called *victim type*.

The idea of the victim or victim type is situational and can vary dependent upon the offense or type of hate crime that is committed. Hate crimes such as aggravated assault or intimidation are crimes against persons and may involve a single victim or multiple victims who were harmed or threatened with harm. When hate crimes are crimes against property such as arson or vandalism, the victim type is based on who owns the property which can expand beyond individuals to other entities or institutions. For instance, the FBI notes that hate crime victimization can occur to individuals, businesses, religious organizations, government entities, or public society (FBI, 2019b). Recognizing that there can are multiple victim types in the conceptualization of hate crime can have an impact on its measurement and should not be overlooked.

Cross-Classification

Hate crime can overlap with other kinds of crime, which can result in its cross-classification or misclassification. Cross-classification refers to recognizing an offense as both a hate crime and another type of crime. Misclassification refers to recognizing the offense as something else but not as a hate crime. The primary concern here is when hate crime is officially misclassified and labeled as something else. This section addresses some of these behaviors that overlap with hate crime.

In some instances, phrases such as terrorism, domestic terrorism, extremism, right-wing extremism are used to label or describe incidents that legally qualify as hate crimes. It is important to realize that even when these alternate labels are used, the incident is still a hate crime provided the elements of bias motivation and a criminal offense are present. Extremism or right-wing extremism are conceptual terms utilized more when the perpetrators are affiliated with an extremist group that is hate-based, such as white supremacy groups (Sullaway, 2016). Terrorism and domestic terrorism are legally defined terms and can be levied as criminal charges. Fortunately, it is not often that hate crime overlaps with these phrases as they most often involve acts of mass violence.

Recent examples of mass violence events include the shootings at the church in Charleston, South Carolina, the Pulse nightclub in Orlando, Florida, the synagogues in Pittsburg, Pennsylvania and Poway, California, the Walmart in El Paso, Texas, and the mass stabbing at a rabbi's home in Monsey, New York. Labeled as acts of domestic terrorism, these incidents are also hate crimes motivated by anti-African American, anti-gay, anti-Jewish, and anti-Latino bias. The connection between hate crime and domestic terrorism have been noted by scholars (Gerstenfeld, 2018). Sullaway (2016) thoroughly explored the distinctions between hate crime, extremism, and domestic terrorism, showing that the overlap could be modeled through a Venn diagram. Policy makers are also aware that hate crime and domestic terrorism can be one in the same. In 2019, the state of New York proposed the "Hate Crimes Domestic Terrorism Act" which would treat and punish acts of mass violence motivated by bias as crimes of terrorism (governor.ny.gov, 2019). The federal government has also responded with a proposed bill that would dedicate federal law enforcement resources to monitor domestic terrorist activity, with focus on white supremacists and right-wing extremists (Domestic Terrorism Prevention Act, 2020). The present trend appears to be cross-categorizing hate crime with domestic terrorism.

Another type of crime which has all the required components of hate crime but is often misclassified is bullying. Bullying involves repeated aggressive behaviors that can include physical force, verbal harassment, relational harm, and property damage, which can be perpetrated directly or indirectly (Gladden, 2014). Instances when bullying involves the use of physical force, verbal threats of harm, or damage of property clearly align with the hate crime offenses of assault (aggravated or simple), intimidation, and destruction, damage or vandalism of property. In addition, bullying or cyber-bullying may be directed towards youths because of their perceived differences based upon sexual orientation, disability, race, ethnicity, national origin, or religion (Englander, 2007; Stopbullying.gov, n.d.). Bias motivation would be established when cases of bullying target youth because of their affiliation with these protected groups. Not to say that all bullying is hate crime but bullying that involves the perpetration of criminal offenses motivated by bias certainly parallels hate crime, yet it is not labelled as such.

Perhaps it is because bullying is typically a behavior that is associated with youth that there is reluctance to qualify it as hate crime. In fact, there is a reluctance to even label such behavior as crime in general. When this type of behavior is committed by adults it is labelled as harassment or cyber harassment and is criminalized behavior handled by the criminal justice system. When this behavior is committed by minors it is labelled as bullying or cyber-bullying and is dealt with through disciplinary actions at school. To classify bullying as a hate crime could increase the severity of punishment for juveniles two-fold, first by treating it as an adult offense and second by elevating to a hate crime.

Scholarly research has begun to recognize that bullying is a "junior" version of hate crime (Englander, 2007). Furthermore, the criminal justice system is beginning to treat bullying as criminal behavior. In 2015, Pennsylvania passed legislation making cyber-bulling of a juvenile a criminal offense. Labeled "cyber harassment of a child," using electronic means to repeatedly make a "seriously disparaging statement or opinion about the child's physical characteristics, sexuality, sexual activity or mental or physical health or condition" is a crime (Pa. Code 18 § 2709.a.1, 2015). This law opens the door to making bullying a hate crime by codifying such behavior as criminal and including elements of bias motivation. Perhaps these paradigm changes on how bullying is viewed will widen the net for the conceptualization of hate crime.

Summary

In this chapter, we have sought to provide information about how hate crime is conceptualized in this country. Hate crime was deconstructed into its bias component and crime component with discussion provided on how each is legally defined. Furthermore, we addressed topics relevant to the conceptualization of bias motivation which included the distinction between bias motivation categories and bias types, how perception and association are linked to bias motivation, and the possibility of intersectionality. In reference to the crime component, we identified common offenses showing the range of behaviors that hate crimes encompass. We explained how different types of criminal offenses can involve different types of victims expanding the idea of the victim beyond just individuals. And lastly, we illustrated how hate crime can be cross-classified or misclassified as other criminal behaviors. All of these topics are pertinent to the conceptualization of hate crime and can impact its measurement.

References

American Psychological Association. (2017). *Multicultural guidelines: An ecological approach to context, identity, and intersectionality.* https://www.apa.org/about/policy/multicultural-guidelines.pdf

Anti-Defamation League. (2019, July). *Anti-Defamation League state hate crime statutory provisions.* https://www.adl.org/media/13726/download

California Penal Code, Ca. P.C. § 422.56. (2019). http://leginfo.legislature.ca.gov/faces/codes_displaySection.xhtml?sectionNum=422.56.&lawCode=PEN

Crime Codes of Pennsylvania, 18 Pa.C.S. § 2709.a.1 Cyber harassment of a child. (2015). https://www.legis.state.pa.us/WU01/LI/LI/CT/HTM/18/00.027.009.000..HTM

Crime Codes of Pennsylvania, 18 Pa.C.S. § 2710 Ethnic intimidation. (2008). https://www.legis.state.pa.us/WU01/LI/LI/CT/HTM/18/00.027.010.000..HTM

Division of Criminal Justice Services. (2019, October). *New York State Uniform Crime Reporting Program: UCR cross-reference table.* Albany, NY: Division of Criminal Justice Services.

Domestic Terrorism Prevention Act, H.R. 1931, 116th Cong. (2020). https://www.congress.gov/bill/116th-congress/house-bill/1931

Englander, E. (2007). Is bullying a junior hate crime? Implications for intervention. *American Behavioral Scientist, 51*(2), 205–212.

Federal Bureau of Investigation. (n.d.). *Defining a hate crime.* https://www.fbi.gov/investigate/civil-rights/hate-crimes#Definition

Federal Bureau of Investigation. (2015). *Hate crime data collection guidelines and training manual.* https://ucr.fbi.gov/hate-crime-data-collection-guidelines-and-training-manual.pdf

Federal Bureau of Investigation. (2019a). *Hate crime statistics, 2018: About hate crime statistics.* https://ucr.fbi.gov/hate-crime/2018/resource-pages/about-hate-crime

Federal Bureau of Investigation. (2019b). *Hate crime statistics, 2018: Methodology.* https://ucr.fbi.gov/hate-crime/2018/resource-pages/methodology

Gerstenfeld, P. B. (1992). Smile when you call me that!: The problems with punishing hate motivated behavior. *Behavioral Sciences & the Law, 10*(2), 259–285.

Gerstenfeld, P. B. (2018). *Hate crimes: Causes, controls, and controversies* (4th ed.). Thousand Oaks, CA: Sage.

Gladden, R. M. (2014). *Bullying surveillance among youths: Uniform definitions for public health and recommended data elements.* Atlanta, GA: Centers for Disease Control and Prevention.

Governor.ny.gov. (2019, August 10). *Governor Cuomo advances first-in-the-nation domestic terrorism law to include mass violence motivated by hate.* https://www.governor.ny.gov/news/governor-cuomo-advances-first-nation-domestic-terrorism-law-include-mass-violence-motivated

Hate Crimes Statistics Act, 34 United States Code §41305. (1990). https://uscode.house.gov/view.xhtml?req=(title:34%20section:41305%20edition:prelim)

LA. Rev. Stat. 14 § 170.2 Hate Crimes. (2016). http://legis.la.gov/legis/Law.aspx?d=78262

Lawrence, F. M. (1999). *Punishing hate.* Cambridge, MA: Harvard University Press.

Levin, J., & McDevitt, J. (1993). *Hate crimes: The rising tide of bigotry and bloodshed.* New York: Plenum.

McDevitt, J., Levin, J., & Bennett, S. (2002). Hate crime offenders: An expanded typology. *Journal of Social Issues, 58*(2), 303–317.

New York Offenses Against Public Order, NYS Penal Law § 240.31. (n.d.). https://www.nysenate.gov/legislation/laws/PEN/240.31

New York Hate Crimes Act, NYS Penal Law § 485.05. (2000). https://www.nysenate.gov/legislation/laws/PEN/485.05

Oudekerk, B. (2019, March 29). *Hate crime statistics.* [PowerPoint slides]. Bureau of Justice Statistics. https://www.bjs.gov/content/pub/pdf/hcs1317pp.pdf

Petrosino, C. (1999). Connecting the past to the future: Hate crime in America. *Journal of Contemporary Criminal Justice, 15*(1), 22–47.

Shanmugasundaram, S. (2018, April 15). *Hate crimes, explained*. SPLC. https://www.splcenter.
    org/20180415/hate-crimes-explained
Southern Poverty Law Center (SPLC). (2017). *Ten ways to fight hate: A community response
    guide*. https://www.splcenter.org/20170814/ten-ways-fight-hate-community-response-guide
Stopbullying.gov. (n.d.). *Who is at risk*. https://www.stopbullying.gov/bullying/at-risk
Sullaway, M. (2016). Hate crime, violent extremism, domestic terrorism – distinctions without
    difference? In *The psychology of hate crimes as domestic terrorism: US and global issues [3
    volumes]* (pp. 89–122). Santa Barbara: Praeger.
U.S. Const. amend. I.
U.S. Const. amend. XIV.

Chapter 3
Hate Crime Data Collection Systems

Abstract This chapter is a review of data collection systems that measure hate crime at a national level. We discuss how hate crime is measured by the UCR Hate Crime Statistics Program and the National Crime Victimization Survey (NCVS), the two primary sources for hate crime statistics, and we include the School Crime Supplement (SCS), the School Survey on Crime and Safety (SSOCS), and the Campus Safety and Security (CSS) reporting system, which measure hate crimes nationally for educational environments. The history of each data collection system is presented respective to the measurement of hate crime. We show how each system defines and operationalizes hate crime, with particular attention given to which bias motivations and criminal offenses are included in the measurement process. Furthermore, we note any important changes to these data collections systems that can impact the measurement of hate crime. Our discussion in this chapter identifies those systems that collect hate crime data in this country, outlining how each measures hate crime, but more importantly, showing how each system measures hate crime differently.

Keywords Bias crime · Bias motivation · Bias types · Criminal offense · Data collection · Hate crime · UCR Hate Crime Statistics Program · National Crime Victimization Survey · School Crime Supplement · School Survey on Crime and Safety · Campus Safety and Security

The purpose of this chapter is to review the current systems that collect data on hate crime at a national level. Discussion will primarily focus on the two major national data collection systems, the UCR Hate Crime Statistics Program and the National Crime Victimization Survey (NCVS). In addition, other federal data collections systems are addressed and include the School Crime Supplement (SCS) to the NCVS, the School Survey on Crime and Safety (SSOCS), and the Campus Safety and Security (CSS) reporting system.

The passage of the Hate Crime Statistics Act (HCSA) of 1990 legally mandated that the federal government begin collecting data on hate crimes in the country.

© The Author(s), under exclusive license to Springer Nature Switzerland AG 2021
F. S. Pezzella, M. D. Fetzer, *The Measurement of Hate Crimes in America*, SpringerBriefs in Criminology, https://doi.org/10.1007/978-3-030-51577-5_3

Initially, this responsibility fell upon the Federal Bureau of Investigation (FBI) which incorporated hate crime data collection into its Uniform Crime Reporting (UCR) Program. Along the way, other federal entities like the Bureau of Justice Statistics (BJS), the National Center for Education Statistics (NCES), and the Office of Postsecondary Education (OPE) began collecting data on hate crime.

Irrespective of the data collection system, the official measurement of hate crime in this country only has a history that spans 30 years. In this chapter we identify and describe systems that measure hate crime in the United States. Later chapters in this book compare these programs, looking at their strengths and limitations in regard to the measurement of hate crime, and present on the patterns and trends of hate crime in this country.

In order to provide useful explanations of these data collection systems, this chapter has several objectives. The first objective is to provide a historical context of each program – when it began and if any changes have been made regarding the measurement of hate crime. A second objective is to describe what the "case definition" is for hate crime in each system, addressing the data collection method and units of analysis. Following along the lines of Chap. 2, how each program defines and operationalizes bias motivations and criminal offense is reviewed. This relates to the last objective of the chapter which is to explain how hate crime is measured by each data collection system. We begin by first discussing the UCR Hate Crime Reporting Program, followed by the NCVS, and then concluding with the systems that collect national hate crime data for schools.

UCR Hate Crime Statistics Program

History

Following the enactment of the Hate Crime Statistics Act in 1990, the first federal agency to collect hate crime data was the FBI, which incorporated hate crime data collection into its already existing Uniform Crime Reporting (UCR) Program. Hate crime data were collected at a national level for the first time in 1992, and the results were presented in the "Hate Crime Statistics, 1992" publication (FBI, 2019c). For the past three decades, the FBI has continued to collect hate crime data through the UCR program and publish it in annual volumes of the "Hate Crime Statistics."

Collection Method & Case Definition

The UCR program collects hate crime data from official police records, which reflect only crimes known to law enforcement agencies. Hate crime data are submitted by law enforcement agencies through one of two systems – the Summary Reporting System (SRS) or the National Incident-Based Reporting System

(NIBRS). Participating law enforcement agencies can report hate crimes either monthly or quarterly directly to the FBI or through their state UCR programs (FBI, 2019d).[1] Individual law enforcement agencies utilize either the SRS or NIBRS to submit crime data to the FBI, but most agencies currently use the SRS (FBI, 2019f). However, it should be noted that the FBI anticipates that NIBRS will be adopted by all law enforcement agencies nationwide by 2021 (FBI, 2019a). NIBRS is a designed improvement to the SRS because it measures more crimes and more details about criminal incidents, however, both systems measure hate crime at an incident-level and collect similar basic details. There are some subtle differences in how each system measures offenses for hate crimes, and NIBRS collects more additional data elements for hate crime incidents. More specific discussion of these differences is given in later sections of this chapter.

For the Hate Crime Statistics Program, the FBI defines hates crime as "criminal offenses that were motivated, in whole or in part, by the offender's bias against the victim's race/ethnicity/ancestry, gender, gender identity, religion, disability, or sexual orientation, and were committed against persons, property, or society" (FBI, 2019d, p. 1). The bias component of a hate crime must be substantiated by law enforcement before the incident can be reported to the FBI. Law enforcement report incidents of hate crime "only if investigation reveals sufficient objective facts to lead a reasonable and prudent person to conclude that the offender's actions were motivated, in whole or in part, by bias" (FBI, 2015, p. 4). Therefore, hate crimes in the UCR program are official reports of criminal incidents known to law enforcement in which bias motivation is substantiated through investigation.

Data on hate crimes are collected at the incident-level, permitting for different units of analysis to be measured. These units of analysis include incidents, offenses, victims, and offenders (CJIS, n.d.). Counts for hate crime may vary dependent upon which unit of analysis is studied. A single hate crime incident may involve one or multiple hate crime offenses, committed by one or multiple hate crime offenders against one or more hate crime victims. The FBI recognizes that individuals, businesses or financial institutions, government entities, religious organizations, or society can be victims of hate crime (FBI, 2019d).

Bias Motivation

The UCR program collects detailed information about bias motivation for hate crimes. Both bias motivation categories and specific bias types are identified for hate crimes. This allows for general bias motivations (e.g., religious bias) to be identified as well as the specific targeted group (e.g., anti-Jewish). The bias motivation categories and bias types define what hate crimes are and how they are measured, and these have changed over the history of the Hate Crime Statistics Program.

---

[1] Participation in the UCR Program is voluntary for state, county, and local law enforcement (CJIS, n.d.) and participating agencies may not submit reports for the entire year (FBI, 2019d).

They have been revised, relabeled, and added to, thus impacting the conceptualization and measurement of hate crime in the United States. Table 3.1 presents the current bias motivation categories and bias types, noting changes that have occurred throughout the Hate Crime Statistics Program.

The definition of hate crime with respect to bias motivation has expanded significantly since the FBI first started collected hate crime data. When the Hate Crime Statistics Program began, only 19 bias types within four bias motivation categories were recognized for hate crimes in the United States. At the time that this book was written, the FBI provides options for six different bias motivation categories and 34 bias types to be identified (see Table 3.1). The original bias motivation categories included race, ethnicity/national origin, religion, and sexual orientation (FBI, 1993). Bias motivation categories for disability, gender and gender identity, along with their respective bias types were added in 1997 and 2013 respectively (FBI, 2019c).

In 2013, several changes were made to the measurement of bias motivations (FBI, 2014). Bias types under the racial motivation category were both revised and relabeled (see Table 3.1). "Black" became "Black or African American" and "Asian or Pacific Islander" was separated into "Asian" and "Native Hawaiian or Other Pacific Islander." "National Origin" was removed from the bias motivation category "Ethnicity/National Origin" to become "Ethnicity," and its bias types of "Hispanic or Other Ethnicity/National Origin" were relabeled as "Hispanic or Latino" and "Not Hispanic or Latino." The last changes included relabeling bias types under sexual orientation with "Anti-Male Homosexual," "Anti-Female Homosexual," and "Anti-Homosexual" becoming "Anti-Gay (male)," "Anti-Lesbian," and "Anti-Lesbian, Gay, Bisexual, or Transgender (Mixed Group)."

The most recent revisions to bias motivation in the UCR program occurred in 2015. Seven additional religious bias types were added including "Anti-Mormon," "Anti-Jehovah's Witness," "Anti-Eastern Orthodox (Russian, Greek, Other)," "Anti-Other Christian," "Anti-Buddhist," "Anti-Hindu," and "Anti-Sikh" (FBI, 2016). These additions weren't necessarily new religions being added as they would have been previously identified as "Anti-Other Religion" in earlier years. Also, in that same year, the bias motivation categories of "Race" and "Ethnicity" were merged and "Ancestry" was created and added making a new bias motivation category of "Race/Ethnicity/Ancestry," to which "Anti-Arab" was added and "Anti-Not Hispanic or Latino" became "Anti-Other Race/Ethnicity/Ancestry" (FBI, 2016). These are a lot of modifications to bias motivation affecting how hate crimes are defined and measured. Many of these changes, particularly the additions of new bias motivation categories, were done to reflect amendments to the Hate Crime Statistics Act.

Intersectionality

The FBI recognizes that hate crime incidents can involve more than one bias motivation or have intersectionality. Incident types are distinguished between single-bias and multiple-bias. A single-bias incident involves "one or more offense types

Table 3.1 UCR Hate Crime Statistics Program bias motivation categories and types

Bias motivation category	Original bias types	Current bias types
Race/ethnicity/ancestry[a] (1990[b], 1992[c])	Anti-white	Anti-white
	Anti-black	Anti-black or African American
	Anti-American Indian or Alaska Native	Anti-American Indian or Alaska Native
	Anti-Asian or Pacific Islander	Anti-Asian[d]
		Anti-Native Hawaiian or other Pacific Islander[d]
	Anti-Multiple Races, Group	Anti-Multiple Races, Group
		Anti-Arab[e]
	Anti-Hispanic	Anti-Hispanic or Latino
	Anti-other ethnicity or national origin	Anti-other race/ethnicity/ancestry[e,f]
Religion (1990, 1992)	Anti-Jewish	Anti-Jewish
	Anti-Catholic	Anti-Catholic
	Anti-Protestant	Anti-Protestant
	Anti-Islamic (Muslim)	Anti-Islamic (Muslim)
	Anti-other religion	Anti-other religion
	Anti-Multiple Religions, Group	Anti-Multiple Religions, Group
		Anti-Mormon[e]
		Anti-Jehovah's Witness[e]
		Anti-eastern orthodox (Russian, Greek, other)[e]
		Anti-other Christian[e]
		Anti-Buddhist[e]
		Anti-Hindu[e]
		Anti-Sikh[e]
	Anti-atheism/agnosticism/etc.	Anti-atheism/agnosticism/etc.
Sexual orientation (1990, 1992)	Anti-male homosexual	Anti-gay (male)[g]
	Anti-female homosexual	Anti-Lesbian[g]
	Anti-homosexual	Anti-LGBT (mixed group)[g]
	Anti-heterosexual	Anti-heterosexual
	Anti-bisexual	Anti-bisexual
Disability (1994, 1997)		Anti-physical disability
		Anti-mental disability
Gender (2009, 2013)		Anti-male
		Anti-female
Gender identity (2009, 2013)		Anti-transgender
		Anti-gender non-conforming

Note: This table presents the original and current bias motivation categories and bias types utilized by the FBI's Hate Crime Statistics Program, indicating when they were added to the program and when data were first reported in the *Hate Crime Statistics* publication. Dates for bias types are the same as those for the corresponding bias motivation categories except where specifically noted
[a]In 2015, the bias motivation categories of Race and Ethnicity were merged and Ancestry was added creating Race/Ethnicity/Ancestry

(continued)

Table 3.1 (continued)

[b]The first year in parentheses reflects when the bias motivation category/type was added to the Hate Crime Statistics Act

[c]The second year in parentheses reflects when data for the bias motivation category/type was first reported in *Hate Crime Statistics*

[d]In 2013, Anti-Asian or Pacific Islander was separated into Anti-Asian and Anti-Native Hawaiian or Other Pacific Islander

[e]These bias types were added to the Hate Crime Reporting Program with data first reported in *Hate Crime Statistics, 2015*

[f]Anti-Other Race/Ethnicity/Ancestry replaced Anti-Not Hispanic or Latino

[g]These bias types were relabeled in 2013

that are motivated by the same bias type", while a multiple-bias incident involves "one or more offense types motivated by two or more bias types" (FBI, 2019d, p. 3). The definition of multiple-bias incidents was revised in 2013 from "an incident in which more than one offense type occurs and at least two offense types are motivated by different biases" (FBI, 2013, p.1) and now allows for five bias motivation types per offense type (FBI, 2019d). Single-bias incident types are counted in their respective bias motivation category and bias type, while multiple-bias incidents are simply designated as such in the "Hate Crime Statistics" publications.

Criminal Offenses

The other component for defining and measuring hate crimes involves which criminal offenses are included. Recall that the HCSA specifies "murder, non-negligent manslaughter; forcible rape; aggravated assault, simple assault, intimidation; arson; and destruction, damage or vandalism of property" as hate crimes (1990). The FBI collects data on these offenses as well as some additional ones when measuring hate crime. In the UCR program, this is one area where differences between the SRS and NIBRS have some impact. Which offenses that can be counted as hate crimes depends upon which of these two systems, the SRS or NIBRS, a law enforcement agency uses.

The FBI collects hate crime data for 13 specific offense types – all the SRS Part I crimes and three Part II crimes. These offense types include murder and non-negligent manslaughter, rape, aggravated assault, simple assault, intimidation, arson, and destruction/damage/vandalism – the HCSA crimes – and the additional offense types of human trafficking–commercial sex acts, human trafficking–involuntary servitude, robbery, burglary, larceny/theft, and motor vehicle theft (FBI, 2019b).[2] These 13 offenses are collected through both the SRS and NIBRS, but NIBRS can collect additional offenses as hate crimes. Table 3.2 displays these offense types and identifies them as either Part I or Part II crimes. This table also

---

[2] In 2013, "human trafficking-commercial sex acts" and "human trafficking-involuntary servitude" were added to the Part I crimes in the SRS and Group A crimes in NIBRS (CJIS, 2013).

Table 3.2 UCR Hate Crime Statistics Program, SRS versus NIBRS offense types

Offense types	SRS	NIBRS
Crimes against persons		
Murder & non-negligent manslaughter	Part I	Group A
Rape[a]	Part I	Group A
Aggravated assault	Part I	Group A
Simple assault	Part II	Group A
Intimidation	Part II	Group A
Human trafficking-commercial sex acts	Part I	Group A
Human trafficking-involuntary servitude	Part I	Group A
Other[b]	–	Group A
Crimes against property		
Robbery	Part I	Group A
Burglary	Part I	Group A
Larceny-theft	Part I	Group A
Motor vehicle theft	Part I	Group A
Arson	Part I	Group A
Destruction/damage/vandalism	Part II	Group A
Other[c]	–	Group A
Crimes against society[d]	–	Group A

Note: The offense types presented in this table represent those collected through the Hate Crime Statistics Program. Information to create this table was compiled from the *Crime in the United States, 2018* (FBI, 2019b), *NIBRS, 2018* (FBI, 2019e), and *Hate Crime Statistics* (CJIS, n.d.)
[a]Rape from NIBRS agencies include the offense types of rape, sodomy, and sexual assault with an object
[b]Other Crimes Against Persons include kidnapping or abduction, fondling, incest, and statutory rape
[c]Other Crimes Against Property include bribery, counterfeiting or forgery, embezzlement, extortion or blackmail, fraud offenses, and stolen property offenses
[d]Crimes Against Society include animal cruelty offenses, drug or narcotic offenses, gambling offenses, pornography or obscene material offenses, prostitution offenses, and weapon law violations

shows additional offenses captured by NIBRS, and categorizes the offense types as crimes against persons, crimes against property, and crimes against society.

NIBRS agencies can report any Group A offense as a hate crime. There are currently 52 Group A offenses in NIBRS, and they are categorized as crimes against persons, crimes against property, and crimes against society (FBI, 2019e). Of the 13 offenses collected by both systems, murder and non-negligent manslaughter, rape, aggravated assault, simple assault, intimidation, human trafficking–commercial sex acts, and human trafficking–involuntary servitude are crimes against persons. NIBRS collects additional crimes against persons, which are simply identified as "Other" in the "Hate Crime Statistics" publications, and include kidnapping or abduction, fondling, incest, and statutory rape (CJIS, n.d.). Crimes against property include robbery, burglary, larceny/theft, motor vehicle theft, arson, and destruction/damage/vandalism. NIBRS captures "other crimes against property" which include bribery, counterfeiting or forgery, embezzlement, extortion or blackmail, fraud offenses, and stolen property offenses (CJIS, n.d.). Additionally, law enforcement agencies utilizing NIBRS are the only ones that can submit crimes against society as hate crimes, which include animal cruelty, drug or narcotic offenses, gambling offenses, pornography or obscene material offenses, prostitution offenses, and weapon law violations (FBI, 2019d). In sum, NIBRS agencies can submit 39 additional offense types as hate crimes compared to agencies using the SRS.

National Crime Victimization Survey

History

The Bureau of Justice Statistics (BJS) is responsible for the second major crime data collection system in the U.S. – the National Crime Victimization Survey (NCVS). Since 1973, the NCVS has collected data on self-reported victimizations from a nationally representative sample of households on an annual basis (Langton, Planty, & Lynch, 2017). The NCVS is viewed as "complementary" to the UCR program in collecting crime estimates for the nation (Morgan & Kena, 2017; Morgan & Oudekerk, 2019). The survey collects information on incidents of crime that are both reported and not reported to law enforcement. Those victimizations not reported to police reflect the "dark figure of crime" and bolster the crime statistics gathered through the UCR program which relies on official police reports. While the NCVS did not initially measure hate crime, BJS eventually developed survey items that would identify victims of hate crime in 1997 which were then implemented in July of 2000 (BJS, 2017; Harlow, 2005; Strom, 2001). Hate crime data has been collected annually since 2003 (BJS, 2017; Masucci & Langton, 2017; Sandholtz, Langton, & Planty, 2013).[3]

Collection Method and Case Definition

The NCVS "collects information on non-fatal crimes against persons age 12 or older from a nationally representative sample of U.S. households" (Morgan & Kena, 2017, p. 1). Every year, the NCVS is administered to approximately 95,000 households in the U.S. and involves approximately 240,000 interviews of about 160,000 individuals (BJS, n.d.). Households are interviewed seven times over a 3-year period, each time inquiring retroactively about victimizations occurring in the previous 6 months (BJS, 2017). Two questionnaires are used at each interview period for the determination and measurement of victimizations. The first questionnaire is a screener that determines if any victimizations occurred in the prior 6-month period

---

[3] Refers to hate crime questions being on the public use file of the NCVS (BJS, 2017, p. 53).

(BJS, 2016a). If a victimization did occur, then a follow up questionnaire – the crime incident report – is administered to collect detailed information about that victimization (BJS, 2016b). Data on criminal victimizations are then weighted to produce national estimates.

The NCVS defines hate crimes as "crimes perceived by victims to be motivated by an offender's bias against them for belonging to or being associated with a group largely identified by these characteristics" (Masucci & Langton, 2017, p. 1; Sandholtz et al., 2013, p. 1). "These characteristics" refer to the bias motivation categories of race, ethnicity, religion, sexual orientation, disability, or gender. Because the NCVS is a self-report survey of victimizations, the offender's bias motivation in perpetrating the crime is determined by the perception of the victim.

Data from the NCVS can studied at different units of analysis – incidents or victimizations. An incident is "a specific criminal act involving one or more victims and offenders" (BJS, 2017, p. 50). However, hate crimes are measured by the NCVS as hate crime victimizations. "Hate crime victimization refers to a single victim or household that experienced a criminal incident believed to be motivated by hate" (Masucci & Langton, 2017, p. 2). The NCVS includes questions that allow for the measurement of both the bias motivation and crime components.

Bias Motivation

Bias motivation in the NCVS is measured as bias motivation categories which include race, religion, ethnic background or national origin, disability, gender, and sexual orientation. Additionally, the NCVS includes bias motivations for perception and association. Respondents are asked a series of questions in the crime incident report to identify bias motivation. This series of questions begins by assessing if the victim perceived that they were targeted because of the offender's bias. If so, the victim is asked questions about the offender's possible bias motivations, and then questions that allow for the corroboration of the offender's bias.

The initial question dealing with hate crimes inquires of respondents as to whether they perceived that they had been targeted because of the offender's bias. The actual language of this survey item is

> Hate crimes or crimes of prejudice or bigotry occur when an offender targets people because of one or more of their characteristics or religious beliefs. Do you have any reason to suspect the incident just discussed was a hate crime or crime of prejudice or bigotry? (BJS, 2016b, p. 33).

This requires the victims to make judgements about the offender's motives and whether they believe that their victimizations were out of prejudice or bigotry. If this is the case, the victims are then asked to indicate which bias categories they perceive to have motivated the offender.

Respondents are asked "Do you suspect the offender targeted you because of … your race, your religion, your ethnic background or national origin, any disability, your gender, or your sexual orientation?" (BJS, 2016b, p. 34). Victims can identify any one or all of these motivations (i.e., a single-bias or multiple-biases) that they perceived to be responsible for the offender's actions. The NCVS also includes bias motivation categories for perception and association (Sandholtz et al., 2013). Although not traditional categories for bias motivation, these are certainly examples of how crimes can be motivated by bias or prejudice (see Chap. 2 for a discussion on this). Respondents are asked if they suspect that they were targeted "because of your association with people who have certain characteristics or religious beliefs (for example, a multiracial couple)" (BJS, 2016b, p. 34). Also, respondents are asked if they feel that they were targeted because of "the offender's perceptions of your characteristics or religious beliefs (for example, the offender thought you were Jewish because you went to a synagogue" (p. 34). So bias motivation in the NCVS includes the eight categories of race, religion, ethnic background or national origin, disability, gender, sexual orientation, perception, and association.

The last sequence of survey items deals with corroborating the victims' perceptions that of crime was motivated by the offender's bias or prejudice. Corroboration of the offender's bias is determined through derogatory language used by the offender, hate symbols left by the offender, or confirmation by law enforcement that it was, in fact, a hate crime. Derogatory language includes if the offender "made fun of the victim, made negative comments, used slang, hurtful words, or abusive language," and hate symbols include examples such as "a swastika, graffiti on the walls of a temple, a burning cross, or written words" (BJS, 2016b, p. 35).

Gender and Gender Identity

Following the passing of the Matthew Shepard and James Byrd, Jr. Hate Crimes Prevention Act in 2009, gender and gender identity were included as bias motivation categories to the Hate Crime Statistics Act. The NCVS had already included gender bias in its original series of questions on the crime incident report, well before modifications to the HCSA (BJS, 2001). However, it was only being reported by BJS when there was an additional bias motivation involved, and following the changes to the HCSA, BJS began reporting on gender bias when they were the only bias motivation in a hate crime victimization (Sandholtz et al., 2013). It should be noted that the NCVS does not inquire about victimization motivated by gender identity bias, but it is possible that such incidents are captured under gender bias if the victim equates gender identity with gender.

Criminal Offenses

The NCVS is used to collect details about victimizations which currently permits for ten separate criminal offenses to be identified. The measurement of victimizations in the NCVS allows for crimes to be differentiated as completed or attempted offenses. These offenses can then be categorized a variety of different ways by BJS and can include personal crimes, violent crimes, serious violent crimes, and property crimes.

The ten criminal offenses presently measured by the NCVS include rape, sexual assault, robbery, aggravated assault, simple assault, purse snatching, pocket picking, household burglary, motor vehicle theft, and theft (BJS, 2017). Similar to the UCR's classifications of crimes against persons and crimes against property, the NCVS classifies crime into two categories: personal crimes and property crimes. Personal crimes include rape, sexual assault, robbery, aggravated assault, simple assault, purse snatching, and pocket picking, while property crimes include household burglary, motor vehicle theft, and theft.[4] Furthermore, personal crimes can be specified as either violent or non-violent; non-violent personal crimes include purse snatching and pocket picking. Any of these criminal offenses can be hate crimes, provided that the victim perceived that the victimization was motivated by bias and there was some corroborating evidence for this. Since hate crimes are measured as victimizations, personal crimes will count a victimization for each victim, and property crimes will count a victimization for each household (Morgan & Kena, 2017).

National Hate Crime Data Collected for Schools

Hate crime data are also collected in the U.S. for sub-populations from academic environments. There are three main data collection systems that identify and measure hate crime for schools. The first of which, is a supplement to the NCVS known as the School Crime Supplement (SCS). The second data collection system is the School Survey of Crime and Safety (SSOCS). Both the SCS and SSOCS measure hate crimes among primary and secondary education populations. The third system collects hate crime data for colleges and universities and is known as the Campus Safety and Security (CSS) reporting system.

School Crime Supplement

Over the history of the NCVS, there have been several supplements or addendum surveys occasionally included once the NCVS is completed. This additional survey, the School Crime Supplement (SCS), measures additional victimization information for school-aged respondents. The SCS was first administered in 1989 by the Bureau of Justice Statistics (BJS) and the National Institute of Justice (NIJ); it was

---

[4] Robbery is classified as a crime against property in the UCR, but a crime against persons in the NCVS.

next administered in 1995 by BJS and the Department of Education's National Center for Educational Statistics (NCES) (U.S. DOJ, 2020). The supplement was again administered in 1999 and has since evolved into a biennial supplement to the NCVS. Bias-motivated victimizations were first measured in the 1999 SCS, and have been measured in every biennial iteration since.

Collection Method and Case Definition

The SCS first utilizes the sampling procedures of the NCVS, and then the SCS is administered to qualifying respondents. Qualifying respondents include individuals between the ages of 12 and 18 who have attended a primary or secondary school in the past 6 months (U.S. DOJ, 2020).[5] The unit of analysis is for the SCS is individuals, and data are collected about victimizations that have occurred at school. The supplement asks questions of individuals that allow for hate crime victimizations at school to be identified and measured.

Bias Motivation

Bias motivation in the SCS parallels most of the categories used in the NCVS. Victimizations could be perpetrated out of bias against the respondent's race, religion, ethnic background or national origin, disability, gender, or sexual orientation (BJS, 2014). The SCS does not include measures to identify bias because of perception or association, which are included in the NCVS. The determination of bias motivation is different from the NCVS due to the types of the victimizations that are measured by the SCS.

Criminal Offenses

The victimizations identified by the SCS are not criminal offenses in the traditional sense. Here victimizations include exposure to hate-related words verbally, and exposure to hate-related words or symbols through graffiti, and bullying. Recall that with the NCVS, criminal victimizations were corroborated as hate crimes through the presence of hate speech or hate symbols. With the SCS, exposure to hate speech or hate symbols, themselves, qualify as victimizations. Whether bullying qualifies as a criminal offense is debatable, and this was discussed conceptually in Chap. 2. Bullying in the SCS includes being made fun of; having rumors spread; being

---

[5] Schools included "public or private elementary schools, middle schools, high schools, church schools, and vocational or trades schools that led to a high school diploma" and persons who were home schooled or attended colleges or universities were excluded (U.S. DOJ, 2020, p. 5).

threatened with harm; physical contact such as being pushed, shoved, tripped, or spit on; coerced to give up money or property; being excluded; and having property destroyed (BJS, 2014). Several of these examples of bullying – threatened with harm; being pushed, shoved, tripped, or spit on; being coerced to give up money or property; and having property destroyed – would be defined as criminal victimizations if they occurred to adults. Furthermore, several iterations of the SCS measured injuries from physical bullying which could include serious harm such as "teeth chipped or knocked out, broken bones, internal injuries, and being knocked unconscious" (BJS, 2008, p. 8). Physical bullying with injuries to this extent would qualify as aggravated assaults. Changes to the supplement in 2015 now allow for victims to report whether they perceived that their being bullied was motivated by their race, religion, ethnic background or national origin, disability, gender, or sexual orientation (BJS, 2014). Thus, the SCS can measure hate-related bullying, exposure to hate-related words, and exposure to hate symbols.

School Survey on Crime and Safety

The second hate crime data collection system for schools is the School Survey on Crime and Safety (SSOCS). The SSOCS is a nationally representative survey of schools, grades K through 12, that gathers data on violence that affects school students and personnel (Diliberti, Jackson, Correa, & Padgett, 2019; Musu, Zhang, Wang, Zhang, & Oudekerk, 2019). The SSOCS is a reoccurring survey conducted by the National Center for Education Statistics (NCES) that has been administered over seven academic years: 1999–2000, 2003–2004, 2005–2006, 2007–2008, 2009–2010, 2015–2016, and 2017–2018. The survey is designed to measure the incidence of crime and violence through questionnaires that are voluntarily completed by school principals. Hate crime has been included as one of the types of crime measured by the SSOCS since its beginning.

Collection Method & Case Definition

The SSOCS utilizes a stratified probability sampling design to obtain a nationally representative sample of primary schools, middle schools, high schools, and combined schools that vary by enrollment size and urbanicity (Diliberti et al., 2019). The survey collects data on indicators of crime and crime prevention strategies from the school level. Hence, the units of analysis are primarily schools, but also incidents when measuring crime. The SSOCS provides estimates for the number of schools that experience hate crime as well as estimates for the number of hate crime incidents. Here, hate crime incidents would only be those that have come to the attention of the school administrators.

Bias Motivation

Since its inception, the SSOCS has defined hate crimes as "a criminal offense or threat against a person, property, or society that is motivated, in whole or in part, the offender's bias against race, color, national origin, ethnicity, gender, religion, disability, or sexual orientation" (Miller, 2003, p. 93). Bias motivations were measured collectively (i.e., "hate crimes") until the 2015–2016 survey was modified to include gender identity, and bias motivations were parsed out to measure race or color, national origin or ethnicity, gender, religion, disability, sexual orientation, and gender identity separately (Diliberti, Jackson, & Kemp, 2017). The measurement of criminal offenses for hate crimes have also undergone modification over the history of the SSOCS. The 1999–2000 SSOCS allowed for specific criminal offenses – rape, sexual battery, physical attack, threats of physical attack, robbery, theft, weapon possession, sexual harassment, and vandalism – to be identified as hate crimes (Miller, 2003). Except for the first year that the survey was administered, the crime component of hate crimes has been measured collectively (i.e., "hate crimes"). All following versions of the SSOCS simply ask respondents to report the number of hate crimes that occurred at their school. From the 2015–2016 survey onward, respondents could indicate yes or no for which bias motivation categories were involved in the hate crimes at their school, but counts are not given for these (Diliberti et al., 2017).

Campus Safety and Security Reporting

The third school-based data collection system that gathers information on hate crimes is the Campus Safety and Security (CSS) reporting system. This program began in 1990, following the passage of the Jeanne Clery Disclosure of Campus Security and Campus Crime Statistics Act (2018), and requires all postsecondary institutions that receive Title IV student financial aid to report annual crime statistics (Musu et al., 2019). The Campus Safety and Security Reporting program is administered by the Department of Education's Office of Postsecondary Education (OPE), which legally mandates that colleges and universities collect and report on all criminal incidents that occur on campus. Four categories of crime statistics are compiled by the CSS reporting program: criminal offenses, VAWA offenses, arrests and referrals for disciplinary actions, and hate crimes (U.S. Department of Education, 2016). Data on hate crimes have been reported since 2009 in the CSS.

The CSS collects data for "on-campus" hate crime incidents that are reported to campus police or security. If an incident involves multiple offenses, all offenses that were motivated by bias are counted. Hate crimes are defined as "a criminal offense that manifests evidence that the victim was intentionally selected because of the perpetrator's bias against the victim" (U.S. Department of Education, 2016, pp. 3–25). Incidents of on-campus hate crime are measured and classified using eight bias motivation categories and 14 criminal offenses. Current bias motivation categories include race, religion, sexual orientation, gender, gender identity, ethnicity, and national origin (U.S. Department of Education, 2016). These bias motivation categories were modified in 2013 by the addition of gender identity and the separation of ethnicity and national origin into their own categories (Clery Center, n.d.). Presently, hate crime offenses include murder and non-negligent manslaughter, rape, fondling, incest, statutory rape, robbery, aggravated assault, burglary, motor vehicle theft, arson, larceny-theft, simple assault, intimidation, and damage, destruction, or vandalism of property (U.S. Department of Education, 2016). Data collected on incidents of hate crime include the institution, criminal offense(s), bias motivation(s), geographic location, and year of occurrence.

Summary

This chapter presented information about five national hate crime data collection systems – the UCR Hate Crime Statistics Program, the National Crime Victimization Survey, the School Crime Supplement, the School Survey on Crime and Safety, and the Campus Safety and Security Reporting Program. We provided information about each systems' history of measuring hate crime, the case definition for a hate crime, and how these phenomena are measured respective to bias motivation and criminal offenses. Each data collection system measures hate crime differently. The UCR Hate Crime Statistics Program is the most inclusive in terms of the number of criminal offenses and bias motivations that are included as hate crimes. However, each of the other national data collection systems provide additional pieces to the puzzle of hate crime in this country.

While we refer to each of these systems as hate crime data collection systems, they are more accurately labeled as data collection systems that measure hate crime. By this we mean that primary purpose of each of these data collection systems is not to measure hate crime. They measure crime and victimization at a much broader scope, but hate crime is included. Even the FBI's Hate Crime Statistics Program is part of the larger UCR program, and law enforcement agencies must first volunteer to participate in the UCR program and then also volunteer to submit hate crime data. Because none of these data collection systems were designed to solely focus on hate crime, there are inherent limitations and inadequacies with their measurement of hate crime. We discuss these limitations in Chap. 4.

References

Bureau of Justice Statistics. (2001). *National Crime Victimization Survey: NCVS-2 crime incident report*. https://www.bjs.gov/content/pub/pdf/quest_archive/ncvs2.pdf
Bureau of Justice Statistics. (2008). *School Crime Supplement to the National Crime Victimization Survey 2009 questionnaire*. https://www.bjs.gov/content/pub/pdf/scs09_q.pdf
Bureau of Justice Statistics. (2014). *School Crime Supplement to the National Crime Victimization Survey 2015 questionnaire*. https://www.bjs.gov/content/pub/pdf/scs15_q.pdf

Bureau of Justice Statistics. (2016a). *National Crime Victimization Survey: NCVS-1 basic screen questionnaire*. https://www.bjs.gov/content/pub/pdf/ncvs18_bsq.pdf

Bureau of Justice Statistics. (2016b). *National Crime Victimization Survey: NCVS-2 crime incident report*. https://www.bjs.gov/content/pub/pdf/ncvs18_cir.pdf

Bureau of Justice Statistics. (2017). *National Crime Victimization Survey, 2016: Technical documentation*. https://www.bjs.gov/content/pub/pdf/ncvstd16.pdf

Bureau of Justice Statistics. (n.d.). *Data collection: National Crime Victimization Survey (NCVS)*. https://www.bjs.gov/index.cfm?ty=dcdetail&iid=245

Clery Center. (n.d.). *Explaining hate crimes under the Clery Act*. http://ncsam.clerycenter.org/wp-content/uploads/NCSAM18_Explaining-Hate-Crimes.pdf

Criminal Justice Information Services. (2013, May 7). UCR program adds human trafficking offenses to data collection, includes more specific prostitution offenses. *CJIS Link, 15*(1). https://www.fbi.gov/services/cjis/cjis-link/ucr-program-adds-human-trafficking-offenses-to-data-collection-includes-more-specific-prostitution-offenses

Criminal Justice Information Services. (n.d.). *Hate crime statistics*. https://www.fbi.gov/services/cjis/ucr/hate-crime

Diliberti, M., Jackson, M., Correa, S., & Padgett, Z. (2019). *Crime, violence, discipline, and safety in U.S. public schools: Findings from the School Survey on Crime and Safety, 2017-18*. NCES 2019-061. National Center for Education Statistics. https://nces.ed.gov/pubs2019/2019061.pdf

Diliberti, M., Jackson, M., & Kemp, J. (2017). *Crime, violence, discipline, and safety in U.S. public schools: Findings from the School Survey on Crime and Safety, 2015-16*. NCES 2017-122. National Center for Education Statistics. https://nces.ed.gov/pubs2017/2017122.pdf

Federal Bureau of Investigation. (1993). *Hate Crimes Statistics, 1992*. https://www.ncjrs.gov/pdf-files1/Digitization/149507NCJRS.pdf

Federal Bureau of Investigation. (2013). *Hate Crimes Statistics, 2012*. https://ucr.fbi.gov/hate-crime/2012/resource-pages/methodology/methodology_final.pdf

Federal Bureau of Investigation. (2014). *Hate Crime Statistics, 2013*. https://ucr.fbi.gov/hate-crime/2013/resource-pages/about-hate-crime/abouthatecrime_final.pdf

Federal Bureau of Investigation. (2015). *Hate crime data collection guidelines and training manual*. https://ucr.fbi.gov/hate-crime-data-collection-guidelines-and-training-manual.pdf

Federal Bureau of Investigation. (2016). *Hate Crime Statistics, 2015: About hate crime statistics*. https://ucr.fbi.gov/hate-crime/2015/resource-pages/abouthatecrime_final.pdf

Federal Bureau of Investigation. (2019a). *A guide to understanding NIBRS*. https://www.fbi.gov/file-repository/ucr/a-guide-to-understanding-nibrs.pdf/view

Federal Bureau of Investigation. (2019b). *Crime in the United States, 2018: Offense definitions*. https://ucr.fbi.gov/crime-in-the-u.s/2018/crime-in-the-u.s.-2018/topic-pages/offense-definitions

Federal Bureau of Investigation. (2019c). *Hate Crime Statistics, 2018: About hate crime statistics*. https://ucr.fbi.gov/hate-crime/2018/resource-pages/about-hate-crime.pdf

Federal Bureau of Investigation. (2019d). *Hate Crime Statistics, 2018: Methodology*. https://ucr.fbi.gov/hate-crime/2018/resource-pages/methodology

Federal Bureau of Investigation. (2019e). *NIBRS, 2018: Crimes against persons, property, and society*. https://ucr.fbi.gov/nibrs/2018/resource-pages/crimes_against_persons_property_and_society-2018.pdf

Federal Bureau of Investigation. (2019f). *NIBRS, 2018: Summary for NIBRS, 2018*. https://ucr.fbi.gov/nibrs/2018/resource-pages/summary.pdf

Harlow, C. W. (2005). *Hate crime reported by victims and police*. Washington, DC: US Department of Justice, Office of Justice Programs, Bureau of Justice Statistics.

Hate Crimes Statistics Act, 34 United States Code §41305. (1990). https://uscode.house.gov/view.xhtml?req=(title:34%20section:41305%20edition:prelim)

Jeanne Clery Disclosure of Campus Security Policy and Campus Crime Statistics Act of 1990, 20 U.S.C. §1092(f) (2018).

Langton, L., Planty, M., & Lynch, J. P. (2017). Second major redesign of the National Crime Victimization Survey (NCVS). *Criminology & Public Policy, 16*(4), 1049–1074.

Masucci, M., & Langton, L. (2017). *Hate crime victimization, 2004–2015.* Washington, DC: US Department of Justice, Office of Justice Programs, Bureau of Justice Statistics.

Miller, A. K. (2003). *Violence in US public schools: 2000 school survey on crime and safety.* Washington, DC: National Center for Education Statistics, US Department of Education, Institute of Education Sciences. https://nces.ed.gov/pubs2004/2004314.pdf

Morgan, R. E., & Kena, G. (2017). *Criminal victimization, 2016.* Washington, DC: US Department of Justice, Office of Justice Programs, Bureau of Justice Statistics.

Morgan, R. E., & Oudekerk, B. A. (2019). *Criminal victimization, 2018.* Washington, DC: US Department of Justice, Office of Justice Programs, Bureau of Justice Statistics.

Musu, L., Zhang, A., Wang, K., Zhang, J., & Oudekerk, B. (2019). *Indicators of school crime and safety: 2018.* https://www.bjs.gov/content/pub/pdf/iscs18.pdf

Sandholtz, N., Langton, L., & Planty, M. (2013). *Hate crime victimization, 2003–2011.* Washington, DC: US Department of Justice, Office of Justice Programs, Bureau of Justice Statistics.

Strom, K. (2001). *Hate crimes reported in NIBRS, 1997–99.* Washington, DC: US Department of Justice, Office of Justice Programs, Bureau of Justice Statistics.

U.S. Department of Education, Office of Postsecondary Education. (2016). *The handbook for campus safety and security reporting, 2016 edition.* https://www2.ed.gov/admins/lead/safety/handbook.pdf

U.S. Department of Justice, Bureau of Justice Statistics. (2020). *National Crime Victimization Survey: School Crime Supplement, 2017* (ICPSR 36982) [Codebook]. ICPSR. https://doi.org/10.3886/ICPSR36982.v1

Chapter 4
Measurement Issues

Abstract This chapter includes an in-depth discussion of measurement issues associated with hate crime data collection. Examples are given from the UCR Hate Crime Statistics Program, the National Crime Victimization Survey (NCVS), and the systems that measure school-based hate crimes to show the impacts of these measurement issues. We begin by addressing issues that arise with the data collection methods, target populations, missing data, geographic scope, temporal issues, and units of analysis. Measurement issues concerning the determination of bias motivation and the offenses that are included as hate crimes are presented. The information that we provide in this chapter is designed to provide and understanding of the strengths and limitations of data collection systems for measuring and studying hate crime.

Keywords Bias categories · Bias motivation · Bias types · Criminal offenses · Data collection · Geographic scope · Hate crime · Instrumentation · Missing data · NCVS · Reference period · Target populations · Temporal issues · UCR · Units of analysis

The purpose of this chapter is to outline and discuss issues with the measurement of hate crime in America. Previous chapters have discussed how hate crimes are conceptualized and the data collection systems used to measure these phenomena at a national level. We build upon this information by delving into issues that arise when operationalizing hate crime. This chapter is organized by topic, addressing various measurement issues and their implications on the accuracy of estimates for hate crime in this country. Topics include issues with the data collection process, and the operationalization of bias motivation and criminal offenses. We explain these measurement issues in reference to the UCR Hate Crime Statistics Program and the National Crime Victimization Survey (NCVS), showing the strengths and limitations of the data collection systems for studying hate crime. Discussion

F. S. Pezzella, M. D. Fetzer, *The Measurement of Hate Crimes in America*, SpringerBriefs in Criminology, https://doi.org/10.1007/978-3-030-51577-5_4

focuses mainly on the UCR program and the NCVS, as these are the two primary systems for collecting hate crime data in the United States, but when relevant, we use examples from the data collection programs that gather data on hate crimes for schools which include the School Crime Supplement (SCS) to the NCVS, the School Survey on Crime & Safety (SSOCS), and the Campus Safety and Security (CSS) reporting system.

Issues with Data Collection

We begin this discussion by focusing on issues surrounding the research designs for the collection of hate crime data. Here, there are several areas where measurement issues can arise which include the method of collection, target population, incomplete or missing data, geographic scope, temporal elements, and units of analysis. Each of these areas are discussed, showing how issues with measurement can impact the accuracy of hate crime data.

Method of Data Collection

The current data collection systems gather information on hate crime through different methods and from different sources, both of which can affect the validity of hate crime estimates for the United States. There are two main methods utilized for the collecting national hate crime data – official records or surveys. The UCR program uses official records from law enforcement agencies while the NCVS collect data on hate crimes through self-report surveys from victims. With official records of hate crimes, law enforcement agencies are limited by their knowledge of these offenses occurring in their jurisdiction. For hate crimes to become known to police, victims must make decisions to report their victimization. Measurement issues arise when victims choose not to report hate crimes to the authorities, as the UCR program is unable to identify these hate crimes. Research has shown that the extent to which victims do not report hate crimes to police is problematic, as victims, unfortunately, are more likely to *not* report their victimization (e.g., Harlow, 2005; Langton & Planty, 2011; Masucci & Langton, 2017; Sandholtz, Langton, & Planty, 2013).

Self-report surveys like the NCVS interview respondents about their victimizations regardless of whether they were reported to the police. The NCVS has the ability to capture hate crimes that "actually occur" – those known to authorities because the victim reported them plus those not reported (i.e., the dark figure of hate crime). Having the capability to measure hate crime victimizations that are both reported and not reported is a significant strength of the NCVS, which permits for a more complete picture of hate crime in America.

Target Populations

When the question is "How much hate crime occurs in America?", the target population should be everyone within the entire United States who has the risk of experiencing a hate crime. Data collection systems can either measure hate crimes for the entire universe (i.e., U.S. population) or use probability sampling techniques to generate nationally representative estimates. Measurement issues occur if individuals within that target population are excluded from the data collection process. This happens when the target population is not actually the entire United States or when restrictions are placed on the sample.

The UCR program measures hate crime for the entire United Sates. This is done by collecting hate crime data from municipal, county, state, college and university, tribal, and federal law enforcement agencies (FBI, 2015). These agencies' jurisdictions, collectively, cover the entire population of United States. Hate crimes reflect those known to law enforcement that are voluntarily reported by participating agencies. There are no restrictions (e.g., victim age or citizenship) that limit the collection of hate crime data through this program.

The target population for the NCVS does not reflect the United States in its entirety. The survey collects hate crime data from a nationally representative sample of households, but sample restrictions limit its coverage of the total U.S. population. The NCVS "excludes persons under age 12; crew members of maritime vessels; armed forces personnel living in military barracks; the homeless; institutionalized persons, such as correctional facility inmates; U.S. citizens residing abroad; and foreign visitors to the United States" (BJS, 2017, p. 4). The parts of the U.S. population that are excluded from the NCVS sample are not inconsequential. The exclusion of children under 12 years of age alone eliminates approximately 48 million persons in the U.S. population (ChildStats.gov, n.d.). As a result from the exclusion of these segments of the U.S. population, the true volume of hate crime in this country will be underestimated.

Incomplete or Missing Data

The completeness of data on hate crime is directly impacted by the level of participation from data reporters. For systems that utilize surveys to collect data, the terminology used is response rates. For collection systems that rely on official records from agencies, this would be referred to as failing to report. Both deal with the issue of incomplete or missing data through not participating in the data collection process. If respondents or agencies do not participate in the data collection process, then the number of hate crimes will be underestimated.

In survey research, missing data is often addressed through discussion of unit response rates for surveys and item response rates for survey questions. The goal is to obtain the highest response rate possible to rule out issues with response bias.

Surveys with lower responses rates have greater chances for response bias and can have issues with the reliability of hate crime estimates. The National Crime Victimization Survey continuously obtains high response rates, especially for a social survey. The 2018 NCVS, for example, had response rates of 73% for households and 82% for respondents (Morgan & Oudekerk, 2019). In addition, the Bureau of Justice Statistics (BJS) utilizing weighting adjustments for hate crime estimates to compensate for nonresponse bias (Masucci & Langton, 2017). This minimizes measurement error and improves the reliability of estimates of hate crime from the NCVS.

Although the UCR Hate Crime Statistics Program is not a survey, it is reliant on voluntary participation from law enforcement agencies for the reporting of hate crime data. For a hate crime to become known to the FBI, law enforcement must properly record and report the incident by participating in the UCR program. Not every law enforcement agency participates in the UCR program, and any hate crimes occurring within the population that they serve will not be measured. The most recent year of UCR data covered approximately 94% of the U.S. population based upon the law enforcement jurisdictions that submitted hate crime reports (FBI, 2019c). This reflects the reality that not all law enforcement agencies submitted hate crime reports for that year. Additionally, of those agencies that do report hate crimes for a given year, they may not submit hate crime reports for every month or all four quarters. The Hate Crime Statistics Program suffers from incomplete coverage both geographically (i.e., not all jurisdictions in the U.S.) and temporally (i.e., not 12 full months for every agency).

Geographic Scope

The discussion here focuses on the geographic scope of hate crime data collection. Geographic scope refers to the spatial areas that a data collection system can provide hate crime statistics for. Acknowledging that the primary goal of measuring hate crime is to determine its occurrence at the national level, additional goals exist such as being able to disaggregate hate crime estimates for smaller geographies in order to study patterns and trends at these levels. Furthermore, factors and conditions for geographic locales within the United States may influence the occurrence and reporting of hate crimes. The FBI points this out stating "valid assessment about crime, including hate crime, are possible only with careful study and analysis of the various conditions affecting each local law enforcement jurisdiction" (FBI, 2019d, p. 7). The ability to study hate crime at localized levels can provide important information for criminal justice officials and legislators to develop interventions and policies. It is beneficial if a hate crime data collection system allows for subnational dissection in order to detect localized patterns and trends. The inability to study hate crime subnationally can be viewed as a measurement issue for data collection systems as it is a limitation to further understanding the nature of hate crime.

The UCR program and the NCVS have the capability to produce estimates for hate crimes at a national scope. The NCVS produces weighted estimates for the occurrence of hate crime at the national level, while the UCR Hate Crime Statistics Program provide actual counts of hate crimes without any estimations performed. Now the question focuses on whether of these data collection systems are capable of observing hate crimes for a smaller geographic scope. Both the UCR program and the NCVS can disaggregate hate crimes for smaller geographic areas, although the NCVS can only do this to a limited degree. Ideally, one would want to be able to study hate crimes at the national, state, and local levels, but this is not possible with both of these data collections systems.

The UCR program can measure hate crime at local levels because data are collected at the "jurisdictional" level. Jurisdictions are law enforcement agencies for municipalities, universities and colleges, counties, states, tribal lands and the federal government (FBI, 2015). Hate crime data can be studied at the jurisdictional level for these individual agencies. The data can also be observed for cities or aggregated to county, state, and national levels. While data from the UCR can be used to study hate crimes at the localized level of jurisdiction, this is not possible with the NCVS. Data from the NCVS does have limited capabilities for subnational estimations of hate crime victimization. Hate crime estimates can be subdivided into the four Census regions of the Northeast, South, Midwest, and West (e.g., Masucci & Langton, 2017). The Bureau of Justice Statistics has long been aware of the importance in being able to estimate victimizations for smaller geographic areas and has taken steps to improve the capacity for subnational estimation of victimization with the NCVS following its 2016 redesign (Langton, Planty, & Lynch, 2017, p. 1064). This sampling redesign will permit for subnational estimation of hate crime victimizations within selected states, metropolitan statistical areas, and cities.

Regarding geographic scope, the UCR Hate Crime Statistics Program maintains the best capability to study hate crimes at various subnational levels. The redesign of the NCVS is a major step towards being able to provide subnational estimation of hate crime victimization. Accompanied by its ability to measure unreported victimizations, this enhances the importance of the NCVS in measuring hate crime.

Temporal Issues

There are several temporal issues with the measurement of hate crime. The first temporal issue deals with the duration or how long hate crime has been measured in this country. Unlike the long-term availability of data on nonbias crimes in this country, data on hate crimes have been available for a much shorter period of time. The second issue concerns the frequency that hate crime data are gathered, referring to whether this is done continuously or just occasionally. To adequately understand changes in hate crime trends, the measurement of hate crime needs to follow a times series fashion and should be done year after year. The last temporal issue addresses the reference time period for hate crime data collection. If hate crimes are to be measured annually, then the reference time period should be a calendar year, but this is not always the case. Each of these temporal issues are presented in reference to the current data collection systems.

Duration and Frequency of Data Collection

Hate crime data for the entire United States has only been collected for the past three decades following the passage of the Hate Crimes Statistics Act in 1990. However, not all the data collection programs that measure hate crime have done so for that length of time. Knowledge about hate crime, including patterns and trends, is limited by when these data collection systems first began measuring bias motivated crime and for the duration that they have done so. Furthermore, the measurement of hate crimes in this country needs to be ongoing, year after year, if changes are to be adequately detected.

Figure 4.1 presents each of the five data collection programs that measure hate crime at a national level, showing when they first began collecting data on hate crime and their coverage over time. The FBI has the longest duration for collecting data on hate crimes beginning in 1992 (FBI, 1993), while the NCVS started measuring hate crime victimization in July of 2000 (BJS, 2017; Harlow, 2005). The UCR Hate Crime Statistics Program and the NCVS collect data on hate crime continuously, year after year. Their length of history for collecting data coupled with consistent annual measurement allow for either data source to be used to study patterns and changes in hate crime over time. For comparison, we show in Fig. 4.1 how the SCS is administered biennially and the SSOCS sporadically. This intermittent collection of hate crime data is not conducive to detecting year-to-year changes or studying trends.

The longer that hate crime is studied, the more that can be learned about it. The relatively brief history of measuring hate crime in the United States has made it difficult to fully understand this phenomenon. The UCR Hate Crime Statistics Program and the National Crime Victimization Survey both have at least two decades of continuous collection of hate crime data at a national level, making them viable sources for studying hate crime trends.

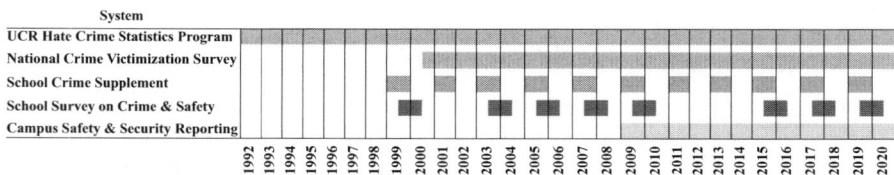

Fig. 4.1 Hate crime data collection systems, coverage by year

Reference Time Period

Preferably, when measuring hate crimes to determine annual patterns and trends the reference time period should be the calendar year and data collection programs should identify all hate crimes that occurred during that span. For instance, the UCR program collects and reports hate crimes for the calendar year, and the number of hate crimes represents those that occurred from January 1st to December 31st of a given year. However, the School Survey on Crime and Safety (see Fig. 4.1) utilizes a reference period of a school year, which is a 12-month period but runs from July of one year to June of the next (Musu, Zhang, Wang, Zhang, & Oudekerk, 2019). It should not be assumed that every national data collection program gathers information or reports hate crimes for the calendar year.

Compared to the UCR program, the reference time period for the NCVS is more complex. The NCVS can define a year two different ways, as a collection year or as a data year. This is because the NCVS is a retrospective survey that collects data on self-reported victimizations that occurred in the past 6 months. The collection year reflects "all crime reported in the year of the interview, regardless of the year that the crime actually occurred," while the data year reflects the year when the crimes occurred (ICPSR, 2020, para. 3). The data year parallels a "calendar year" in that it includes crimes that occurred from January 1st to December 31st. Data users can choose between the 2 year formats, but consumers of BJS publications are limited to the year format used in the specific report. BJS annual publications subscribe to the collection year and special reports (e.g., hate crime) utilize data year (ICPSR, 2020).

While it might seem straightforward that the reference time period for the annual collection of hate crime data would be a calendar year, consumers and producers of research should exert a degree of caution that this may not be true. The reference time periods for each of the data collection systems have been addressed here to provide awareness of this issue.

Units of Analysis & Counts

One of the main goals in measuring hate crime is to determine its frequency of occurrence in the population. This involves counting the number of hate crimes in the United States. While this would seem simple and straightforward, the reality is quite complex and dependent upon what is actually being counted. From a measurement standpoint, counting hate crimes is dependent upon the units of analysis for which data is collected and the type of frequency measure that is used for estimation (i.e., incidence or prevalence). Incidence refers to the number of phenomena, and prevalence refers to the number of persons who experience the phenomena (Centers for Disease Control and Prevention, 2012). With respect to hate crime, incidence would be the number of hate crimes that occur in a population, prevalence would be the number of victims of hate crime. The type of frequency measure is further complicated by the units of analysis for which data is collected. Counts for hate crimes will vary depending upon the unit of analysis is being measured. The units of analysis can differ among hate crime data collections programs, and a single program may collect data for different units of analysis. This is a measurement issue that directly impacts the counts of hate crimes.

The UCR Hate Crime Statistics Program collects incident-level data on hate crimes, which permits for the multiple units of analysis – incidents, offenses, victims, and offenders – to be studied and counted (FBI, 2019e). Counts will vary depending upon which unit of analysis is used. In 2018, for example, the FBI reported 7,120 hate crime incidents involving 8,496 hate crime offenses perpetrated by 6,266 known offenders against 8,819 hate crime victims (FBI, 2019e). So how much hate crime there is in the U.S. varies based upon the unit of analysis and type of frequency measure.

With the NCVS, the primary unit of analysis for measuring hate crime is victimizations, which are defined as "a single victim or household that experienced a criminal incident believed to be motivated by hate" (Masucci & Langton, 2017, p. 2). Counts for victimizations are dependent upon the type of victim (i.e., victims or households) and the type of crime. For personal crimes, the count of hate crime victimizations is equal to the number of individuals who were victimized, but for property crimes, the victimization count is equal to number of households (Bureau of Justice Statistics, 2017). How the NCVS counts hate crimes respective to the type of victim raises a measurement issue when compared to the UCR program.

For property crimes in the NCVS only one victim, the household, is counted despite how many household members might have technically been affected by the crime. In the UCR, crimes against property can include more than one individual. Consequently, the number of victims for property crimes in the NCVS is a 1 to 1 ratio, but in the UCR it can be 1 to many. The UCR program also has a more inclusive definition of a victim which can include "an individual, a business or financial institution, a government entity, a religious organization, or society or the public as a whole" as (FBI, 2019d, p. 4). In 2018 businesses, government entities, religious organizations, and society accounted for approximately 15% of hate crimes in the UCR (FBI, 2019f). The NCVS misses this portion of hate crime by not measuring victimizations for businesses, government entities, religious organizations, or society. Subsequently, the UCR program's more comprehensive definition of a hate crime victim and how victims are counted relative to property crimes results in more hate crimes being counted compared to the NCVS.

What is currently known about the amount of hate crime in America comes primarily from the UCR Hate Crime Statistics Program and the National Crime Victimization Survey. Because the UCR and NCVS both collect incident-level information about hate crimes, multiple units of analysis can be counted and studied. In addition, different measures of frequency, such as incidence, prevalence, and risk, can be estimated. These are strengths that should not be overlooked because there is dimensionality to hate crime (e.g., criminal offenses, victims, and offenders), and these two systems can measure these different dimensions. The various units of analysis and measures of frequency allows for hate crime to be counted in different ways depending on the purpose. If the purpose is to know how many hate crimes occur in the U.S., then measuring incidence would be preferred and the number of offenses or victimizations would be counted. If the purpose is to understand how many persons experience hate crime, then prevalence should be measured, and the number of victims should be counted.

Issues Measuring Bias Motivation

The determination of bias motivation is key to measuring hate crime. The ability to identify those offenses that are motivated by bias and rule out those that are not is essential for being able to accurately measure hate crimes. The measurement of bias motivation should also allow for the bias motivation category to be determined (e.g., racial or religious bias) and the specific bias type (e.g., anti-African American or anti-Jewish) to be identified. The process of identifying and determining bias motivation is the source of several measurement issues, which can impact the accuracy of hate crime estimates.

Who Determines Bias Motivation?

The determination of bias motivation in a criminal offense requires being able to ascertain what an offender's mentality and rationale for the perpetration of their crimes. In some instances, this may be straightforward as the offender presents evidence allowing for the clear substantiation of bias motivation, but in many instances, this may not be the case. Who decides that an offense was a hate crime and how this is done can lead to errors in measurement.

With crimes known to police, law enforcement determine an offense as a hate crime when "investigation reveals sufficient objective facts to lead a prudent person to conclude that the offender's actions were motivated, in whole or in part, by bias" (FBI, 2015, p. 4). Here, law enforcement identify and determine hate crimes through investigation and the gathering of evidence. There is, of course, room for error here. It is possible that an offense was motivated by hate, but law enforcement are unable to substantiate any bias motivation through an investigation. This also operates under the assumption that law enforcement will record and report hate crimes once they have been identified.

The determination of bias motivation by police through an investigation is the method utilized in the UCR program. To support accurate identification of crimes with bias motivation, the UCR program recommends a "two-tier decision-making process" in which a responding officer (i.e., first-level judgement officer) will flag an incident suspected to be motivated by bias and forward it to a person or unit (i.e., second-level judgement officer/unit) trained in hate crime investigations for final determination of bias motivation (FBI, 2015).

The NCVS has a different process for determining bias motivation. The NCVS determines victimizations to be hate crimes based on the victims' beliefs or suspicions that "the offender selected them for a victimization because of one or more of their personal characteristics" (Harlow, 2005, p. 2). Corroborating evidence is required to substantiate the victims' perceptions that the crime was motivated by bias. This evidence includes the "offender's use of hate language, hate symbols left at the scene, or the police investigator's confirmation that a hate crime occurred" (Langton & Planty, 2011). The most common corroborating evidence for hate crimes in the NCVS is hate language, present in almost 99% of hate crime victimizations (Masucci & Langton, 2017).

In either method used by the UCR or NCVS for determining bias motivation there is the possibility for measurement error in identifying hate crime. The investigative requirements for law enforcement are designed to assist in identifying bias-motivation if present, but the inability to find evidence substantiating bias does not necessarily mean the offense was not actually a hate crime. The conservative nature of this process lends itself to the underestimation of hate crimes. Surveys relying on the perceptions of victims may be more likely to identify bias-motivation when it isn't present. The NCVS requires corroborating evidence, but in most instances, this is derogatory language used by the offender. It is entirely possible that victims may misinterpret the language used by the offender as biased. The accuracy of hate crime data can be impacted by either of methods used to identify bias motivation.

How Bias Is Measured

The purpose for measuring bias motivation should be considered when collecting data on hate crimes. If the purpose is to simply identify bias crimes, then a simple indicator for the presence or absence of bias could be used. However, a major justification for having hate crime laws and measuring hate crimes is because people are targeted because of their characteristics or group membership. Thus, the purpose should be to measure bias motivation with enough detail so that characteristics or group membership can be identified. Most data collection systems fail to do this and merely measure broad bias motivation categories (e.g., race, ethnicity, religion, disability, sexual orientation, gender, or gender identity). While this measurement issue doesn't necessarily impact the identification of hate crimes, it does impact the ability to identify patterns and trends for certain groups that are targeted for hate crimes.

The UCR Hate Crime Statistics Program is the *only* data collection system that measures bias motivation with enough detail to identify specific targeted groups. The FBI (2015) can categorize hate crimes into bias motivation categories as well as 34 different bias motivation types (See Table 3.1 in Chap. 3). For example, a hate crime that targeted an individual because they were African American would be identified as having a bias motivation category of race and a bias motivation type of Anti-African American. By measuring bias motivation types, the UCR program can identify the specific targeted group.

The NCVS can only measure bias with enough detail to identify and differentiate hate crimes into bias motivation categories but not bias types. This significantly hinders understanding the nature of hate crime. For example, using NCVS data Massuci and Langton (2017) show that racial bias was the most common motivation for hate crimes from 2011 to 2015. It cannot be determined if one racial group is being targeted more than others, or if hate crime victimizations changed for certain races over that 5-year period. The inability to identify bias motivation by type prohibits the identification of patterns and trends for hate crimes among targeted groups.

Furthermore, there is a measurement issue with the bias motivation categories used by the NCVS. The survey measures bias motivation for the categories of race, religion, ethnic background or national origin, disability, gender, and sexual orientation *but not* gender identity (BJS, 2014, 2017). The exclusion of bias motivation categories such as gender identity will impact the estimation of the occurrence of hate crimes.

Instrumentation

The last measurement issue concerns instrumentation, which is a change in the measurement process (Maxfield & Babbie, 2018). Here, instrumentation occurs when data collections systems modify how bias motivation measured, and this change can have effects on determining the volume of hate crime as well as its patterns and trends. This is most evident with the UCR program, which has modified how bias motivation was measured to reflect changes in the Hate Crime Statistics Act (HCSA). Initially, the UCR program only counted hate crimes motivated by race, ethnicity, religion, and sexual orientation; in 1997 disability bias was added; gender and gender identity were added in 2013; and ancestry was added in 2015 (FBI, 2019c). Each of these expansions to how bias motivation was measured resulted in more hate crimes being counted and impacted trend data. For example, an increase in total hate crimes from 2012 to 2013 might not reflect an actual increase in hate crimes in the country but could be attributed modifying bias motivation to include gender and gender identity in 2013. The instrumentation of bias motivation is a measurement issue that can result in "false" increases in hate crime that are due to *new* hate crimes being counted not *more* hate crimes occurring.

The UCR program has undergone the most changes because it has measured hate crime the longest and because it is directly impacted by changes to the HCSA. Amendments to the HCSA also led to changes in the NCVS. The Bureau of Justice Statistics did not technically modify how the NCVS measured bias motivation, but it did modify how bias motivation was reported. Bias motivation in the NCVS has always included categories for race, ethnic background or national origin, religion, disability, sexual orientation, and gender; however, gender bias was not reported in BJS hate crime publications until after 2009 when the HCSA was amended. Sandholtz et al. (2013) showed the impact that including gender bias had on the overall volume of hate crimes in the NCVS, increasing hate crime estimates by 13,200 victimizations in 2011. Altogether, the effects of instrumentation with bias motivation have resulted in more hate crimes being recognized and impact the validity of trends across years when modifications were made.

Issues Measuring Crime

Which Offenses to Include

Which offenses that are recognized as hate crimes can pose two measurement issues. First, this directly impacts the frequency of hate crimes that will be measured. More offense types will equal more hate crimes or vice versa. Second, the inclusion or exclusion of certain offenses can directly impact the understanding of the nature of hate crime. The capacity to measure a spectrum of criminal offenses permits for patterns and trends to be studied within the umbrella of hate crime.

The UCR program measures more offenses as hate crimes than any other data collection system. However, the offenses that can be classified and reported as hate crimes vary based on whether law enforcement agencies utilize the Summary Reporting System (SRS) or the National Incident-Based Reporting System (NIBRS) for data submission. Both the SRS and NIBRS measure 13 offenses as hate crimes which include murder and non-negligent manslaughter, rape, aggravated assault, simple assault, intimidation, human trafficking–commercial sex acts, human trafficking–involuntary servitude, robbery, burglary, larceny/theft, motor vehicle theft, arson, and destruction/damage/vandalism (FBI, 2019a). These offenses address hate crimes against persons and property as well as non-violent and violent, both fatal and nonfatal, hate crimes. Agencies that currently use NIBRS have the capacity to include 39 additional criminal offenses as hate crime (see Table 3.2 *Notes*). Collectively, the offenses measured through the UCR program provide the broadest picture of the nature and diversity of hate crimes in the United States.

The crimes measured by the NCVS overlap substantially with the UCR program. The NCVS collects victimization data on the crimes of rape, sexual assault, aggravated assault, simple assault, purse snatching, pocket picking, household burglary, theft, and motor vehicle theft. Although these ten offenses are redundant to those measured by the UCR, the NCVS will measure more of these offenses because both crimes reported and non-reported to police are identified by the survey. Masucci and Langton (2017) presented evidence that more than half of hate crimes collected by the NCVS were not reported to the police. By default, the NCVS will measure more offenses because of volume of unreported hate crimes. The capability of the NCVS to measure unreported crimes is one of its biggest strengths, which contributes significantly to the measurement of hate crime.

Although the NCVS will identify more hate crimes through its capacity to measure unreported crimes, a sizeable portion of hate crime is not captured due to the offenses that it excludes. Compared to the UCR program, the NCVS does not measure homicide, arson, human trafficking, intimidation, vandalism, or any of the additional offenses identified through NIBRS. The fact that the NCVS does not measure intimidation and vandalism is significant, as these two offenses count for almost 60% of the hate crime reported through the UCR program (Masucci & Langton, 2017). Consequently, the NCVS fails to measure a substantial portion of hate crime in the United States.

This discussion on which offenses are included under the hate crime umbrella show just how broad of a concept hate crime is. To accurately measure hate crime, a multitude of criminal offenses need to be included. In the end, neither the UCR program nor the NCVS measure all hate crimes, but each system contributes to the overall picture of hate crime.

Instrumentation

Instrumentation is also an is for the measurement of criminal offenses. Data collection systems have been modified in terms of *what* offenses are measured as hate crimes and *how* offenses are measured. The UCR program has modified which offense are included as hate crimes and how offenses are measured. In 2013, two human trafficking offenses, commercial sex acts and involuntary servitude, were incorporated into UCR data collection (CJIS, 2013). This expanded hate crime in the UCR resulting in more offense types being measured than had been prior. The FBI also modified the definition of rape which was incorporated into the UCR program starting in 2013. The new definition of rape removed the required element of force, included males as victims, and merged three offenses: rape, sodomy, and sexual assault with an object (CJIS, 2012). Essentially, the redefining of rape changed how it was measured *and* added offenses (i.e., sodomy and sexual assault with an object) to be counted as hate crime. This resulted in the more than twice as many hate crimes of rape being measured using the revised definition compared to the previous definition (FBI, 2014).

The NCVS has remained relatively consistent in the measurement of criminal offenses, with one major exception. In 2008, vandalism questions were dropped from the survey (BJS, 2017). Vandalism is one of the most prevalent hate crime offenses, particularly among hate crimes against property. When vandalism was measured by the NCVS, it was estimated that approximated 22,500 hate-related vandalisms occurred annually (Harlow, 2005). The removal of vandalism from the NCVS is impactful on measurement of overall hate crime, particularly since the survey can assess the extent of unreported hate crime.

The impact of instrumentation can be clearly seen with examples from the UCR program and the NCVS. Modifying which offenses are measured or how they are measured impacts hate crime counts, the amount of detail collected, and the ability to accurately assess trends across periods prior to and after modifications are made.

Net Widening

With additional offense types being added over the years and variations in which crimes are measured by the various data collection systems, there is a "net widening" effect that has occurred with the measurement of hate crime. The definition of hate crime has broadened in scope in terms of its composition of criminal behaviors. Whether this has a positive or negative impact on the measurement of hate crime is debatable. On one hand, including criminal behaviors motivated by bias that have previously been excluded as hate crimes will enhance the accuracy and understanding of hate crime. On the other side of the debate, this net widening might be including behaviors that are not "criminal" as hate crimes.

Examples can be found in the current data collection programs to support arguments for and against widening the scope of behaviors recognized as hate crime. First, there are some illustrations of how including additional types of crimes improve the measurement of hate crime. The UCR program's inclusion of the 39 additional NIBRS offenses adds to our understanding of the scope and nature of hate crime. The recognition that society or the public as a whole can be the victim of hate crimes warrants the inclusion of these offenses. As more agencies transition to NIBRS, the information from measuring crimes against society and additional crimes against persons and property will become more informative while increasing the number of hate crimes measured by the UCR Hate Crime Statistics Program.[1] Another example is the UCR program's inclusion of human trafficking offenses are an addition to types of criminal offense recognized as hate crime. Human trafficking offenses, particularly those involving commercial sex acts, can involve victims who were targeted because of their gender. Measuring these offenses is both relevant and important to the study of hate crime.

The other side of the debate is that net widening may go too far and include behaviors that are not technically criminal as hate crimes. Illustrations of this can be found with the measurement of sexual harassment as a hate crime by the SSOCS (Miller, 2003) and exposure to hate speech, exposure to hate symbols or graffiti, and bullying by the SCS. Again, the issue is whether these behaviors qualify as criminal offenses or as bias incidents. If the purpose of data collection is to measure legally defined hate crimes, then these behaviors should be excluded.

Summary

This chapter outlined and discussed measurement issues with data collection and the measurement of bias motivation and criminal offenses. It is important to understand the strengths and limitations of the UCR program and NCVS in reference to

---

[1] The FBI anticipates that all law enforcement agencies will transition to NIBRS by 2021 (FBI, 2019b).

measuring and understanding hate crime. Furthermore, comprehension of the issues and nuances with the measurement of hate crime will permit for more informed policy making and responses by the criminal justice system.

No single data collection system is perfect in its measurement of hate crime, nor does any single program fully measure the amount of hate crime in the United States. However, the NCVS and the UCR can be used together in order to gain a better understanding of the phenomenon of hate crime.

References

Bureau of Justice Statistics. (2014). *School Crime Supplement to the National Crime Victimization Survey 2015 questionnaire.* https://www.bjs.gov/content/pub/pdf/scs15_q.pdf

Bureau of Justice Statistics. (2017). *National Crime Victimization Survey, 2016: Technical documentation.* https://www.bjs.gov/content/pub/pdf/ncvstd16.pdf

Centers for Disease Control and Prevention. (2012). *Principles of epidemiology in public health practice: An introduction to applied epidemiology and biostatistics.* Atlanta, GA: U.S. Department of Health and Human Services, Centers for Disease Control and Prevention (CDC), Office of Workforce and Career Development.

ChildStats.gov. (n.d.). *Child population: Number of children (in millions) ages 0–17 in the United States by age.* https://www.childstats.gov/americaschildren/tables/pop1.asp

Criminal Justice Information Services. (2012, March 19). UCR program changes definition of rape: Includes all victims and omits requirement of physical force. *CJIS Link, 14*(1). https://www.fbi.gov/services/cjis/cjis-link/ucr-program-changes-definition-of-rape

Criminal Justice Information Services. (2013, May 7). UCR program adds human trafficking offenses to data collection, includes more specific prostitution offenses. *CJIS Link, 15*(1). https://www.fbi.gov/services/cjis/cjis-link/ucr-program-adds-human-trafficking-offenses-to-data-collection-includes-more-specific-prostitution-offenses

Federal Bureau of Investigation. (1993). *Hate Crimes Statistics, 1992.* https://www.ncjrs.gov/pdf-files1/Digitization/149507NCJRS.pdf

Federal Bureau of Investigation. (2014). *Hate Crime Statistics, 2013: Table 2: Incidents, offenses, victims, and known offenders by offense type, 2013.* https://ucr.fbi.gov/hate-crime/2013/tables/2tabledatadecpdf/table_2_incidents_offenses_victims_and_known_offenders_by_offense_type_2013.xls

Federal Bureau of Investigation. (2015). *Hate crime data collection guidelines and training manual.* https://ucr.fbi.gov/hate-crime-data-collection-guidelines-and-training-manual.pdf

Federal Bureau of Investigation. (2019a). *Crime in the United States, 2018: Offense definitions.* https://ucr.fbi.gov/crime-in-the-u.s/2018/crime-in-the-u.s.-2018/topic-pages/offense-definitions

Federal Bureau of Investigation. (2019b). *A guide to understanding NIBRS.* https://www.fbi.gov/file-repository/ucr/a-guide-to-understanding-nibrs.pdf/view

Federal Bureau of Investigation. (2019c). *Hate Crime Statistics, 2018: About hate crime statistics.* https://ucr.fbi.gov/hate-crime/2018/resource-pages/about-hate-crime.pdf

Federal Bureau of Investigation. (2019d). *Hate Crime Statistics, 2018: Methodology.* https://ucr.fbi.gov/hate-crime/2018/resource-pages/methodology

Federal Bureau of Investigation. (2019e). *Hate Crime Statistics, 2018: Table 2 Incidents, offenses, victims, and known offenders by offense type, 2018.* https://ucr.fbi.gov/hate-crime/2018/topic-pages/tables/table-2.xls

Federal Bureau of Investigation. (2019f). *Hate Crime Statistics, 2018: Table 6 Offenses: Victim type by offense type, 2018.* https://ucr.fbi.gov/hate-crime/2018/resource-pages/tables/table-6.xls

Harlow, C. W. (2005). *Hate crime reported by victims and police*. Washington, DC: US Department of Justice, Office of Justice Programs, Bureau of Justice Statistics.

Hate Crimes Statistics Act, 34 United States Code §41305. (1990). https://uscode.house.gov/view.xhtml?req=(title:34%20section:41305%20edition:prelim)

Inter-university Consortium for Political and Social Research. (2020). *Resource guide: National Crime Victimization Survey*.

Langton, L., & Planty, M. (2011). *Hate crime, 2003–2009*. Washington, DC: US Department of Justice, Office of Justice Programs, Bureau of Justice Statistics.

Langton, L., Planty, M., & Lynch, J. P. (2017). Second major redesign of the National Crime Victimization Survey (NCVS). *Criminology & Public Policy, 16*(4), 1049–1074.

Masucci, M., & Langton, L. (2017). *Hate crime victimization, 2004–2015*. Washington, DC: US Department of Justice, Office of Justice Programs, Bureau of Justice Statistics.

Maxfield, M. G., & Babbie, E. R. (2018). *Research methods for criminal justice and criminology*. Boston: Cengage.

Miller, A. K. (2003). *Violence in U.S. public schools: 2000 school survey on crime and safety*. Washington, DC: National Center for Education Statistics, US Department of Education, Institute of Education Sciences. https://nces.ed.gov/pubs2004/2004314.pdf

Morgan, R. E., & Oudekerk, B. A. (2019). *Criminal victimization, 2018*. Washington, DC: US Department of Justice, Office of Justice Programs, Bureau of Justice Statistics.

Musu, L., Zhang, A., Wang, K., Zhang, J., & Oudekerk, B. (2019). *Indicators of school crime and safety: 2018*. https://www.bjs.gov/content/pub/pdf/iscs18.pdf

Sandholtz, N., Langton, L., & Planty, M. (2013). *Hate crime victimization, 2003–2011*. Washington, DC: US Department of Justice, Office of Justice Programs, Bureau of Justice Statistics.

Chapter 5
Patterns and Trends of Hate Crime in America

Abstract This chapter presents hate crime patterns and trends using data from the UCR Hate Crimes Statistics Program and the National Crime Victimization Survey (NCVS). Comparisons are made between these two data collection systems, noting where the NCVS and UCR agree and differ in findings regarding the occurrence of hate crime. We observe overall and recent trends from the UCR data for all hate crime, and for hate crimes separated into bias motivation categories, bias types, and offense types. Using data from the NCVS, we show patterns among hate crime victims and offenders. We exhibit how the strengths of each of these data collection systems can be utilized to better understand the nature and scope of hate crime in the United States.

Keywords Bias categories · Bias motivation · Bias types · Criminal offenses · UCR · NCVS · Patterns · Trends · Victims · Offenders

This chapter presents patterns and trends for hate crime in the United States. Data from both the UCR Hate Crime Statistics Program and the National Crime Victimization Survey (NCVS) are used, as these are the two primary sources of information of hate crime at a national level. In this chapter, we discuss patterns and trends for the hate crime as a whole, broken down by bias motivations and offense types, and for both victims and offenders. The purpose is to provide information about the nature and occurrence of hate crimes across the nation.

The Volume of Hate Crime

How much hate crime exists in the United States depends on who is doing the measuring. The UCR Hate Crime Statistics Program and the NCVS differ greatly in terms of the volume of hate crime that occur annually. Much larger estimates are

© The Author(s), under exclusive license to Springer Nature Switzerland AG 2021
F. S. Pezzella, M. D. Fetzer, *The Measurement of Hate Crimes in America*, SpringerBriefs in Criminology, https://doi.org/10.1007/978-3-030-51577-5_5

produced by the NCVS compared to the UCR program. Masucci and Langton (2017) show the average number of hate crimes from the UCR to be 8,370 compared to 252,630 from the NCVS. This variance in number of annual hate crimes is due to differences in the design and scope of these data collection systems. These methodological differences have been previously addressed in this book, and they show that both the UCR and the NCVS underestimate the volume of hate crime in this country. The much larger estimate from the NCVS demonstrates how the UCR program's counts of hate crimes known to police fails to measure a sizeable volume of hate crimes that are not reported to police. However, the NCVS fails to measure a sizeable portion of hate crimes by not including relevant offense types such as intimidation and vandalism (Masucci & Langton, 2017). The conclusion is that the amount of hate crimes occurring in the United States is not accurately measured. Despite the lack of agreement about the volume of hate crime, data from both the UCR and NCVS can be used to study its patterns and trends provided that each program measures hate crime consistently over time.

Trend data from both data collection systems show that hate crime in this country has been declining. Data from the NCVS shows an overall downward trend for hate crime, with victimizations decreasing by 26% from 2004 to 2015 (Masucci & Langton, 2017; Sandholtz, Langton, & Planty, 2013). UCR hate crime data confirms that hate crimes have been declining (see Fig. 5.1). While the overall trend for hate crimes is downward, recent data show that hate crimes are on the rise in this country. In the past 5 years hate crimes reported in the UCR have increased by 31% from 6,727 victims in 2014 to 8,819 victims in 2018. While the UCR program and the NCVS differ on the volume of hate crime, they do concur on the overall trending pattern of its occurrence.

Figure 5.1 displays hate crime trends from the UCR for its different units of analysis for measuring hate crime – incidents, offenses, victims, and known offenders. While the trends for these four units of analysis are almost identically parallel, there are differences in terms of the number of hate crimes measured. We use Fig. 5.1 to demonstrate how the unit of analysis impacts the measurement of the volume of hate crime. A common metric for measuring crime is by incident, but a criminal incident can involve multiple offenses, victims, or offenders. Figure 5.1 shows that incidents underestimate the occurrence of hate crime and would not be the best unit of analysis. The number of offenders is typically lower than the number of incidents, so using offenders as the unit of analysis also underestimates hate crime. While there can be more offenders than incidents, these counts are often lower because these are "known offenders," indicating that some aspect of the offender has been identified (FBI, 2019b). In many crimes, especially for crimes against property, the offender or offenders cannot be identified. Relative to the number of incidents, the number of offenses measures more hate crimes. On average, using offenses as the unit of analysis measures approximately 18% more hate crimes. This, of course, is because hate crime incidents can involve multiple offenses. Measuring hate crimes by victims produces the largest counts of hate crimes because the UCR Hate Crime Statistics Program can count multiple victims for property crimes. On average, utilizing victims as the unit of analysis captures

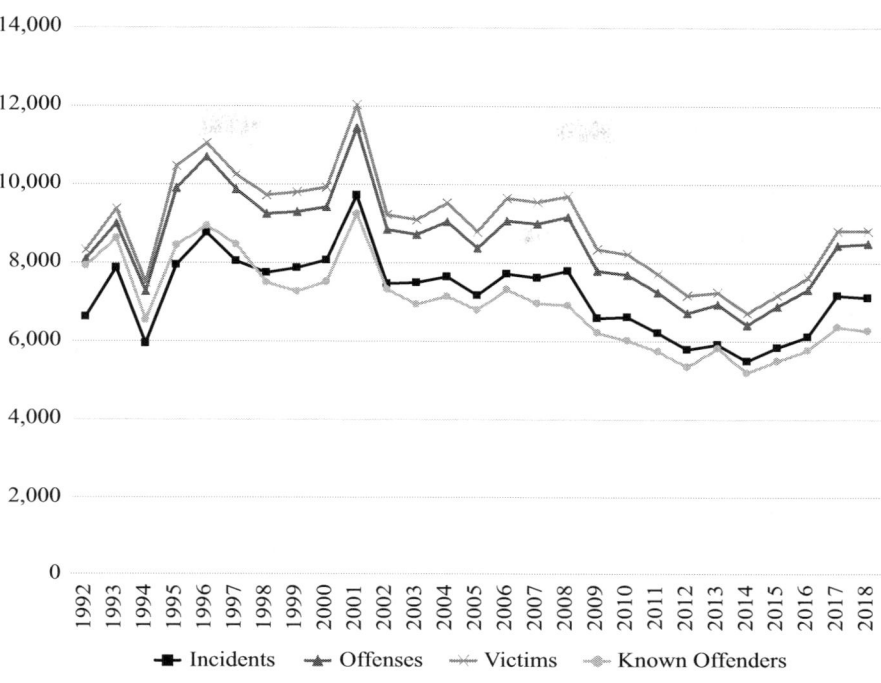

Fig. 5.1 Hate Crime Trends by Unit of Analysis, UCR 1992–2018. *Note*. This figure shows hate crime trends for different units of analysis including incidents, offenses, victims, and known offenders. Data are from the annual *Hate Crime Statistics* publications

24% more hate crimes compared to incidents. Because hate crime incidents can involve multiple offenses and hate crime offenses can involve multiple victims, measuring hate crime with victims as the unit of analysis seems to be a more accurate reflection of the volume of hate crime. Thus, in this chapter we employ victims as the measure for hate crimes from the UCR Hate Statistics Program.

Patterns of Bias Motivation

Going beyond the determination of how much hate crime occurs in the United States, the next important question to address is why victims are targeted. This requires analyzing hate crimes and identifying patterns among the various bias motivations. Ideally, patterns should be able to identify which groups are targeted most often. We first compare bias motivation categories between the UCR and NCVS, highlighting areas of consensus and difference. We then utilize data from the UCR to identify patterns and trends among bias motivation categories and types.

Bias Motivation Categories

Bias motivation categories reflect the broader classes of bias (e.g., race, religion, sexual orientation). While patterns among bias motivation categories are informative, they do lack detail in terms of identifying groups targeted by hate crimes. The NCVS lacks the capability to identify bias motivation for hate crimes beyond the broader categories to specify targeted groups. As such, comparisons between the UCR and NCVS are restricted to categories of bias motivation.

Patterns

Bias motivation patterns are not completely identical between the UCR and the NCVS due to differences in methodologies and measurement. However, when similar patterns are found between these two sources there is confidence as to their validity. When there is divergence between the UCR and the NCVS, decisive conclusions about bias motivation patterns are difficult and require further investigation to explain these differences. Figure 5.2 presents a comparison between the UCR and NCVS for bias motivation categories. To account for any possible fluctuations in

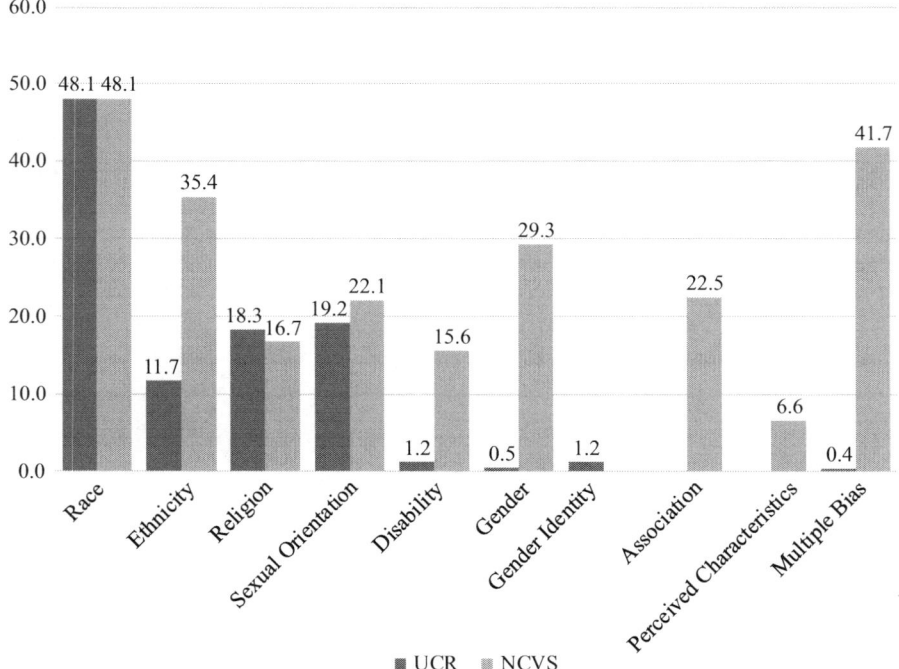

Fig. 5.2 Hate Crime Bias Motivation Categories, UCR versus NCVS 2011–2015

bias motivation patterns for a single year, and to make comparisons as equitable as possible, hate crime data were used for a five-year period, 2011–2015.

During this time period, the UCR and NCVS both concur about hate crimes motivated by race, religion, and sexual orientation. Race is the most prevalent bias motivation for hate crimes in the United States. From 2011 to 2015, almost half of all hate crimes were motivated by racial bias (FBI, 2012; 2013; 2014; 2015; 2016; Masucci & Langton, 2017). Data from the UCR and NCVS report that approximately 1 in every five hate crimes involve bias against religion or sexual orientation. Beyond these three bias motivation categories, patterns greatly differ between the NCVS and UCR. Substantially greater proportions of hate crimes are motivated by ethnicity (35.4% vs. 11.7%), disability (1.2% vs. 15.6%), and gender (0.5% vs. 29.3%) as reported by the NCVS. Relative to the UCR, NCVS prevalence estimates are more than three times greater for ethnicity, 10 times greater for disability, and 60 times greater for gender motivated hate crimes.

Possible explanations for the large differences between the NCVS and UCR in terms of bias motivations could be explained by methodological differences. Data from the UCR reflect those crimes known to police, whereas the NCVS will measure unreported hate crimes. One of the contributing factors for the NCVS's larger proportion of hate crimes motivated by disability bias may be due to victims not notifying police. For instance, Langton and Planty (2011) have shown that victims of hate crimes motivated by disability were the least likely to report their victimization to police. Another explanation contributing to these differences is that multiple bias motivations are much more prevalent in the NCVS than in the UCR. Figure 5.2 shows that 42% of hate crime victimizations in the NCVS reported multiple bias motivations compared to less than 1% of the hate crimes reported through the UCR. This factor can explain the higher percentage of ethnicity bias in the NCVS. Using NCVS data from 2011 to 2015, we found that among hate crimes in which victims reported racial bias 47% of these victims also indicated ethnicity bias. Many victims may view bias motivations against race and ethnicity as too closely related to be distinguish from each other and report them in tandem. The remarkable difference between the UCR and the NCVS in terms of gender bias should not be overlooked. It is possible that how the NCVS corroborates bias motivation using derogatory language by the offender may partially explain this disparity, such that victims may misinterpret the offenders' language as bias motivated intent. While we offer possible explanations for the discrepancies between data sources bias motivations, the extent of these differences for ethnicity, disability, and especially gender certainly warrants further investigation.

Trends

We used data from the UCR Hate Crime Reporting Program found in the "Hate Crime Statistics" annual publications from 1992 to 2018 to observe trends among bias motivation categories. Victims were chosen as the unit of analysis to capture the largest counts of hate crimes from the UCR program. These data were chosen over the NCVS for two reasons. First, the UCR Hate Crime Reporting Program has the longer history of measuring hate crime in this country, providing a longer time period for study. Second, the UCR program has the capability of looking at bias motivation by specific types which allows for targeted groups to be identified. Data for the bias motivation were used to observe both overall and recent trends over the past five years (see Table 5.1).

Recall from Fig. 5.1 that the trend for reported hate crimes in this country shows an overall decrease with signs of an increase in recent years. Similar trends were found for hate crimes when bias motivation is separated into categories for race, ethnicity, and religion. However, fewer racially-motivated hate crimes are reported

Table 5.1 UCR Hate Crime Trends by Bias Motivation Categories and Select Bias Types

Bias Motivation	First Year of Data		Overall Trend		2014 (N)	2018 (N)	Last 5 Years	
	Year	N	Trend	R^2			Increase	% Change[a]
Race	**1992**	**5213**	**Decreasing**	**0.686**	**3227**	**4050**	**823**	**25.5%**
Anti-Black or African American		2948	Decreasing	0.553	2022	2426	404	20.0%
Anti-White		1729	Decreasing	0.625	734	1038	304	41.4%
Ethnicity	**1992**	**865**	**Decreasing**	**0.031**	**821**	**1105**	**284**	**34.6%**
Anti-Hispanic or Latino		508	Decreasing	0.072	389	671	282	72.5%
Anti-Other Race/ Ethnicty/Ancestry		357	Decreasing	0.025	432	334	−98	−22.7%
Religion	**1992**	**1260**	**Decreasing**	**0.006**	**1140**	**1617**	**477**	**41.8%**
Anti-Jewish		1103	Decreasing	0.594	648	920	272	42.0%
Anti-Islamic (Muslim)		17	Increasing	0.269	184	236	52	28.3%
Sexual Orientation	**1992**	**972**	**Increasing**	**0.094**	**1248**	**1445**	**197**	**15.8%**
Anti-Gay (Male)		678	Decreasing	0.019	703	863	160	22.8%
Anti-LGBT (Mixed Group)		138	Increasing	0.548	305	360	55	18.0%
Disability	**1997**	**12**	**Increasing**	**0.702**	**96**	**179**	**83**	**86.5%**
Anti-Mental Disability		3	Increasing	0.584	70	111	41	58.6%
Gender	**2013**	**30**	**Increasing**	**0.707**	**40**	**61**	**21**	**52.5%**
Anti-Female		25	Increasing	0.407	28	33	5	17.9%
Gender Identity	**2013**	**33**	**Increasing**	**0.827**	**109**	**189**	**80**	**73.4%**
Anti-Transgender		25	Increasing	0.963	69	160	91	131.9%
Multiple Bias	**1994**	**4**	**Increasing**	**0.291**	**46**	**173**	**127**	**276.1%**

Note. This table presents data for overall and recent trends for all bias motivation categories and the most prevalent bias types within these categories from the UCR Hate Crime Statistics Program. Overall trends reflect patterns over time from when the bias catoegory/type was first reported in the annual *Hate Crime Statistics* publications through 2018. Recent trends reflect data from the past 5 years, 2014–2018
[a]Percent change is calculated using the formula (Time$_2$ – Time$_1$)/Time$_1$

now than when the UCR program first began in 1992, decreasing from 5,213 in 1992 to 4,050 in 2018 for a −22% change.[1] Hate crimes motivated by bias against sexual orientation, disability, gender, and gender identity each show overall increasing trends. From 1992 to 2018, the number of hate crime victims targeted because of their sexual orientation has increased by 49%, from 972 to 1,445 victims. When disability bias was first measured by the UCR program 1997 there were 12 hate crimes reported. The most recent data for 2018 show 179 reported hate crimes with disability bias. Gender and gender identity were first included in the UCR program in 2013 with 30 and 33 hate crimes reported, respectively. In 2018, the number of reported hate crimes against gender increase by more than 100% to 61 and gender identity increased by more than 400% to 189. Although reported hate crimes motivated by sexual orientation, disability, gender, and gender identity bias have increased over the years, they are fewer in number compared to hate crimes with bias motivations like race. The overall decreasing trend for hate crimes collectively is driven by sheer volume of racially motivated hate crimes, and it is not until hate crime are broken down by bias motivation categories that different trends emerge.

Recent trend data show that each bias motivation category for UCR hate crimes has experienced a dramatic increase. The actual year that recent increases began varies slightly depending on the category, with some as early as 2014 or as recent as 2017. Thus, we present recent trends over the past 5 years for bias motivation categories. Table 5.1 displays these bias motivation trends showing counts for 2014 and 2018, the number that hate crimes increased, and the percent change from 2014 to 2018. In the past 5 years hate crimes in the U.S. have increased by hundreds of victims for the bias motivations of race (+823), ethnicity (+284), religion (+477), and sexual orientation (+197). Given that total hate crimes increased by 2,092 from 2014 to 2018, these four bias motivation categories account for 85% this number with religious bias explaining almost a quarter of this increase. While disability, gender, and gender identity bias did not experience as large increases in volume, they did experience much larger percent increases in this five-year period. Hate crimes of disability bias increased by 87%, gender bias by 53%, and gender identity bias by 73%. Hate crimes reported with multiple bias motivations had the largest percent increase (276%) more than tripling in volume from 46 in 2014 to 173 in 2018. The data show that hate crimes have increased markedly for each bias motivation category. The next step is to show what can be learned by looking within these categories at specific bias motivation types.

---

[1] Percent change is calculated using the formula $(Time_2 - Time_1)/Time_1$.

Bias Motivation Types

The UCR Hate Crime Statistics Program currently identifies 34 bias motivation types included within the broader bias motivation categories (see Table 3.1 from Chap. 3). These bias motivation types provide for more specificity in the measurement of hate crimes and allow for targeted groups to be identified. In order to discuss patterns and trends surrounding bias motivation types, we again used data from the UCR "Hate Crime Statistics" for the past 5 years, 2014–2018 (FBI, 2015, 2016, 2017, 2018, 2019a). We first present patterns of hate crimes by bias motivation types, showing prominently targeted groups within each bias motivation category as well as which bias types are most prevalent overall. We then discuss trends for bias motivation types of hate crime.

Patterns

The ability to measure the bias motivation of hate crimes by type of bias is much more informative than simply using categories for bias motivation. For example, previous discussion identified racial bias as the primary category for hate crimes in the United States, but patterns concerning which race or races are targeted most could not be determined. Bias motivation types allow for patterns to be observed for specific races. Being able to determine which groups are most often targeted is very valuable for research purposes as well as for policy responses. We present some of this information here.

The UCR Hate Crime Statistics Program measures hate crimes for bias motivation categories of race, ethnicity, religion, sexual orientation, disability, gender, and gender identity.[2] By utilizing bias motivation types, patterns for the prevalence of specific groups within each of these categories can be identified. For instance, African Americans and Whites are most often targeted within racially motivated hate crimes. African Americans account for more than half of victims of hate crimes with racial bias, and Whites are victims in approximately 20% of these crimes. Two groups comprise the majority of victims in hate crimes with religious bias. More than half of these victims are Jewish and about 20% are Islamic or Muslim. Most hate crimes based upon one's actual or perceived ethnicity are committed against Hispanic or Latino victims. Among hate crimes targeting persons because of their sexual orientation, 60% of reported bias types are anti-gay male and about 25% are anti-LGBT involving a mixed group of victims. The predominant groups targeted because of bias against disability, gender, and gender identity are persons with mental disabilities, females, and transgendered persons, respectively. When hate crimes are measured by specific bias types, enough information exists to determine which

---

[2] In 2015, the UCR program merged the bias motivation categories of race and ethnicity (FBI, 2019a).

groups are most often targeted within categories of bias. Which groups are most often targeted among all hate crimes can also be determined.

In UCR data, eight of 34 current bias motivation types account for almost 80% of all hate crimes (see Fig. 5.3). These eight bias types show that hate crimes are most often motivated by bias against race, religion, sexual orientation, and ethnicity. From 2014 to 2018, 40% of all hate crimes were racially motivated and involved anti-Black or African American and anti-White bias types. African Americans are, by far, the most often targeted group, accounting for almost 30% of all hate crimes in this country. White victims are the second most targeted group accounting for approximately 11% of hate crimes. A substantial volume of hate crime is motivated by religious bias against persons of the Jewish (11%) and Islamic (4%) faiths. Among these eight bias types, two involve sexual orientation bias and include anti-gay (10%) and anti-LGBT (4%) hate crimes. Anti-Hispanic or Latino (6%) and anti-other race, ethnicity, or ancestry (4%) hate crimes comprise the remainder of these eight bias motivation types. The UCR program's ability to measure bias motivation by type makes it possible to identify which groups are most often targeted for hate crimes. The data show that African Americans are the most targeted group in the United States because of racial bias. Whites are also often targeted because of race, persons of the Jewish and Islamic faiths are often targeted because of religious bias, gay men and mixed groups (i.e., anti-LGBT) due to bias against sexual orientation, and Hispanic persons or persons of other backgrounds (i.e., anti-other race/ethnicity/ancestry) because prejudice against their ethnicity.

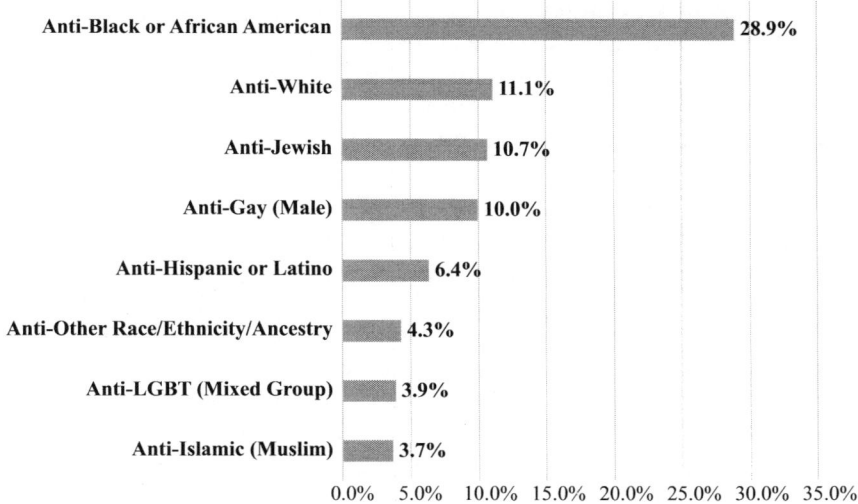

Fig. 5.3 The Eight Most Prevalent Bias Motivation Types for Hate Crimes from the UCR, 2014–2018. *Note.* This figure presents eight of the thirty-four bias motivation types identified in the UCR Hate Crime Statistics Program. These eight bias types account for 79% of all hate crimes reported in the annual *Hate Crime Statistics* publications for 2014 through 2018

Trends

Studying hate crimes trends over the course of the UCR Hate Crime Statistics Program's existence is somewhat difficult for bias motivation types due to instrumentation over the years (see Chap. 4 for a discussion on this). In some instances, this poses concern as to whether trends represent actual changes in the occurrence of hate crimes or reflect changes in the measurement process. When discussing trends, we note any the instances where this may be any issue.

Hate crime trends are presented for the major bias motivation types within each of the categories of race ethnicity, religion, sexual orientation, disability, gender, and gender identity. Overall trends were observed for bias motivation types for all years that data were available, as well as recent trends over the past five years, from 2014 to 2018 (See Table 5.1). Differing patterns over time emerge for hate crimes when bias motivation categories are separated into specific bias types. Some trends for bias types reflect those observed for their broader bias category. For example, hate crimes motivated by bias against race, ethnicity, and religion showed overall decreasing trends. Likewise, anti-Black or African American, anti-White, anti-Hispanic or Latino, and anti-Jewish hate crimes have all shown overall declining trends. Increasing trends were observed for hate crimes with sexual orientation, disability, gender, and gender identity bias. Within these categories, anti-LGBT-mixed group, anti-mental disability, anti-female, and anti-transgender hate crimes have also shown steady growth over the years. Sometimes trends for bias types are the opposite of what was found for the general bias motivation category. For instance, hate crimes based on bias against religion showed an overall decrease, but anti-Islamic hate crimes have been steadily increasing.

While overall trends of hate crime victimization are informative, recent trends can show the current experiences for members of groups targeted in bias crimes. Using the UCR data from 2014 to 2015, we observed contemporary changes in hate crime victimization among bias types.

UCR data show a different picture of hate crimes for these bias types when looking at the past 5 years, from 2014 to 2018. Of the eleven bias motivation types previously discussed, all but one has shown increased victimization over the past 5 years (See Table 5.1). Among the bias types that have experienced recent growth, several have seen substantial increases in frequency, percent change, or both. In this five-year period, anti-Hispanic or Latino increased by 282 (+73%), anti-White by 304 (+42%), and anti-Jewish increased by 272 (+42%). Hate crimes against transgendered persons and individuals with mental disabilities occur in lesser volume, but these have increased by 132% and 58%, respectively in the past 5 years. The one bias type mentioned earlier that did not increase in the last 5 years was anti-other race, ethnicity, or ancestry. The decrease in anti-other race, ethnicity, or ancestry hate crimes may be due to instrumentation. This bias type was constructed in 2015 at the same time when the bias type of anti-Arab was created. We assume that prior to 2015 anti-Arab hate crimes were included in the measurement of anti-other race, ethnicity, or ancestry (formerly anti-Not Hispanic or Latino ethnicity). So, while anti-other race, ethnicity, or ancestry hate crimes have decreased in the past 5 years, anti-Arab hate crimes have increased and more than doubled.

The ability to study hate crimes by specific bias type allow for the detection of these varying patterns for different targeted groups that might be missed if hate crime is simply measured collectively or broken down by just bias motivation categories. The differing patterns over long periods of time reflect the experiences for victims belonging to different targeted groups. Recent trends show that hate crimes are on the rise across most targeted groups, while some groups have experienced greater victimization in the last 5 years.

Patterns & Trends of Hate Crime Offenses

Data from the UCR Hate Crime Statistics Program are primarily used for the discussion on patterns and trends among hate crime offenses. The UCR data were chosen over the NCVS due to the UCR's measurement of more offense types and additional types of victims (e.g., businesses, religious organizations, government institutions, and society). However, some discussion of NCVS hate crime offenses is incorporated when warranted. The UCR program collects hate crime data for 13 offense types from law enforcement agencies that use the Summary Reporting System (SRS) and 52 offense types – the thirteen collected through SRS plus an additional 39 offense types - from agencies that use the National Incident Based Reporting System (NIBRS) (See Table 3.2 from Chap. 3 for a list of these offenses). These 13 criminal offense types are murder and non-negligent manslaughter, rape, aggravated assault, simple assault, intimidation, human trafficking–commercial sex acts, human trafficking–involuntary servitude, robbery, burglary, larceny/theft, motor vehicle theft, arson, and destruction/damage/vandalism; and the additional NIBRS offenses are classified as other personal crimes, other property crimes, and crimes against society (FBI, 2019c). The NCVS only measures crimes that overlap with seven of the thirteen UCR offense types collected from SRS and NIBRS agencies, and these include rape, aggravated assault, simple assault, robbery, burglary, theft, and motor vehicle theft.

Despite the difference in offense types measured between the UCR and NCVS, similar patterns are found for hate crime when observing categories of crime. If hate crimes are categorized as violent (crimes against persons) or non-violent (crimes against property), both data sources conclude that most hate crimes are violent and committed against persons. The proportion of hate crimes that are violent is much higher in the NCVS (89%) than in the UCR (60%) data (Masucci & Langton, 2017). The proportional differences are due to additional offense types measured by the UCR program.

Looking at just the offense types measured by the UCR program, almost all hate crimes involve four offenses types (see Fig. 5.4). Among hate crimes reported from 2014 to 2018, approximately 90% involved vandalism (27%), intimidation (27%), simple assault (22%), or aggravated assault (12%) (FBI, 2015, 2016, 2017, 2018,

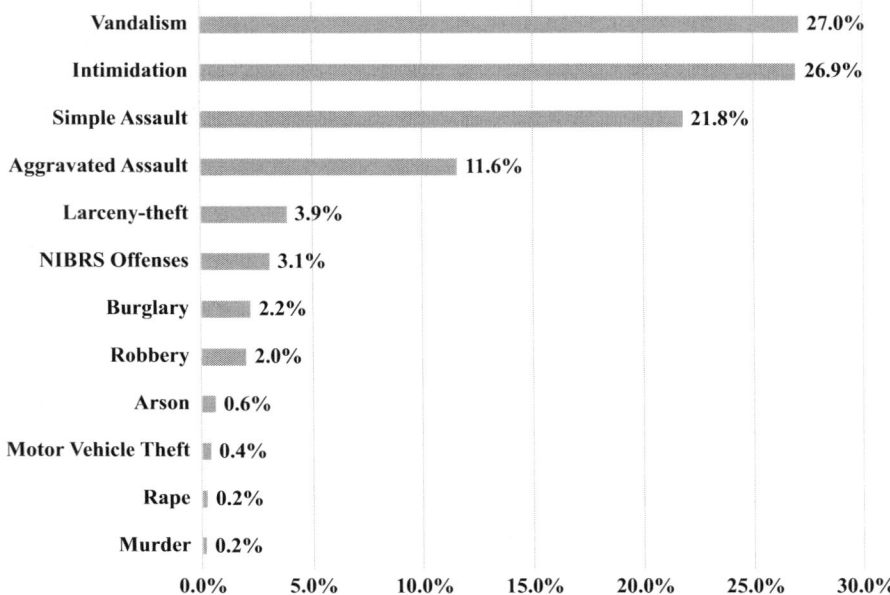

Fig. 5.4 Hate Crimes by Offense Type, UCR 2014–2018

2019a). More than half of all hate crimes reported through the UCR program were the offenses of vandalism and intimidation; two offense types not measured by the NCVS. The remainder of hate crimes included larceny-theft (3.9%), the additional NIBRS offenses (3.1%), burglary (2.2%), robbery (2.0%), motor vehicle theft (0.4%), rape (0.2%), and murder (0.2%). The two offenses types that are viewed as the most serious, murder and rape, are also the most infrequent. During this five-year period, there were 70 hate crime murders and 90 bias-motivated rapes reported. Murder is the rarest hate crime offense type reported by law enforcement agencies. Annual counts of murder in the UCR data are often in the single-digits and has not exceeded 20 cases until 2018, with 24 cases reported.

The overall trend for hate crime murders has been relatively static, except for this recent increase in 2018. Aggravated assaults, simple assaults, intimidations, robberies, arsons, and vandalisms have shown general declining patterns over the history of the UCR program's measurement of hate crimes. Since 1992, overall increasing trends have been found among the offense types of rape, burglary, larceny-theft, motor vehicle theft, and the additional NIBRS offenses.[3]

Recent trends, from 2014 to 2018, show that hate crime collectively is on the rise. Hate crimes against persons have increased by more than 1,500 (+38%) cases. Crimes against property have also gone up but not to the same degree, increasing by 13% (+340 cases). When looking at individual offense types, all except burglary

[3] Noting that rape was redefined and broadened in scope in 2013, we restricted trend data to 2012 and still found an overall increasing trend.

have shown growth over the past 5 years. Reported hate-related burglaries decreased by 20% from 2014 to 2018. Hate crime murders increased six-fold from 4 to 24 in 2018. Under the revised definition, hate crimes of rape have more than doubled from 9 victims to 22. The substantial growth of crimes against persons over the five-year period is from the UCR's assaultive offenses of aggravated assault, simple assault, and intimidation which increased by 256, 381, and 815 hate crimes, respectively. In fact, hate crimes of intimidation have experienced most growth in frequency during this time period. The other major offense type among UCR reported hate crimes, intimidation, rose by 9% from 1,907 cases in 2014 to 2,080 in 2018. Over the past 5 years, the additional NIBRS offenses (i.e., other personal crimes, other property crimes, and crimes against society) have almost quadrupled collectively. Although the recent growth in hate crimes among the additional NIBRS offenses follows the trends found among most other offense types, there should be awareness to the fact that some of this growth is reflected by law enforcement agencies switching from SRS to NIBRS.

There is significant utility in being able to study hate crime by offense types. Patterns can be identified for determining which offense types are more prevalent (e.g., vandalism, intimidation, simple assault, and aggravated assault), and which types are rare (e.g., rape and murder). Recent patterns provide information about the direction that hate crimes are currently moving, and unfortunately the data show that most offense types are on the rise. Of particular concern is the trend that the violent, assaultive offenses of aggravated assaults, simple assaults, and intimidations are occurring with great frequency. Since 2003, vandalism offenses were the most frequent hate crime offense type. Over the course of the past several years, the number of intimidations has increased to the point that in 2018 there were more of these offense types reported than vandalisms, 2,560 versus 2,081. Hate crimes appear to be becoming more violent, and offenders are targeting persons more than property. The awareness of these patterns and trends leads to the search for explanations as to why hate crime is increasing and creating policies and interventions to combat this problem

Victim & Offender Patterns

Knowledge of the bias motivations and offense types is paramount in understanding hate crime, but it is also of great importance to learn about the persons involved in these acts. There will be two parties involved in hate crimes – the victims and the offenders. It is important to discern who the victims of hate crime are and if there are risk factors for being victimized. Information about the victims of hate crime primarily come from NCVS data. The UCR program has always been focused on the offenses and the offenders, often overlooking the victims of crimes. This remains true for the UCR Hate Crimes Statistics Program which collects minimal information about victims (i.e., victim counts and types of victims). However, data collection through NIBRS involves gathering detailed information about victims, but

NIBRS coverage is currently not national.[4] If and when all law enforcement agencies switch to NIBRS, then more comprehensive information about victims should be available. For now, the best source of information of victims is the NCVS.

The NCVS focuses on measuring crime from the victim's perspective. Among the information collected by the NCVS are multiple victim characteristics which can be used to identify patterns and risk factors among hate crime victims. Patterns are observed for the victims' gender, race and ethnicity, age, income, and location of residence. Risk factors are determined by calculating victimization rates for victim characteristics and identifying those with higher rates or risk of victimization.

Gender patterns among hate crime victims have changed over time in the NCVS. Earlier estimates from 2003 to 2011 show that the majority of victims are male, who also experienced higher rates of victimization than females (Langton & Planty, 2011; Sandholtz et al., 2013), however, more recent data show that the gender gap in hate crime victimization has almost become equal (Masucci & Langton, 2017). In terms of race and ethnicity, the majority of hate crime victims are non-Hispanic Whites (53%) and approximately one-quarter were Hispanic, yet Hispanic persons experience higher rates of victimization (Masucci & Langton, 2017). Hate crime victims tend to be younger persons. The largest proportion of hate crime victims are 24 years of age or younger (Sandholtz et al., 2013). Furthermore, juveniles have the highest risk for victimization (Langton & Planty, 2011; Sandholtz et al., 2013; Wilson, 2014). Patterns have also been found based upon victims' income levels. Among household income levels when reported, a large percentage of victims make less than $25,000 a year (Masucci & Langton, 2017). Individuals in this household income bracket have also experienced the highest annual rates (Wilson, 2014). How much money a person makes or doesn't make can influence their risk for hate crime victimization. Where an individual lives can also impact their risk for being a victim of hate crime. Harlow (2005) and Masucci and Langton (2017) found that persons who reside in urban areas experience higher rates of victimization compared to those who live in suburban or rural locations. This is probably a reflection of population density and proximity to more potential offenders. Patterns from NCVS data on hate crime victimizations show that victims tend to be males, non-Hispanic Whites, youth, and persons making lower incomes. Risk factors include being male, Hispanic, juvenile, making less income, and living in cities.

The NCVS also collects information about offender characteristics as reported by victims of hate crimes. These characteristics include typical demographic characteristics (e.g., gender, race, and age), the number of offenders involved in a hate crime, the relationship to the victim, whether the offender used a weapon or injured the victim, and whether the offender was under the influence when the crime was committed. No different from most crimes, males primarily tend to be the perpetrators of hate crimes. Research has shown that approximately 70% of offenders are male (Harlow, 2005; Langton & Planty, 2011; Sandholtz et al., 2013). The race of

---

[4] NIBRS agencies comprised 44% of the law enforcement agencies reporting crime data to the 2018 Uniform Crime Reports and only covered a population of approximately 117 million persons (FBI, 2019d).

hate crime offenders is similar in the proportion of Whites compared to African Americans; however, relative to offenders of non-bias crimes, hate crime offenders are significantly less likely to be White and more likely to be African American (Masucci & Langton, 2017). Compared to non-bias crimes, offenders are more likely to be strangers that are not known to the victim (Masucci & Langton, 2017). Most hate crime offenders act alone yet hate crimes have been shown to be more likely to be committed by multiple offenders when compared to non-bias crimes (Harlow, 2005; Masucci & Langton, 2017). Weapon use and injuring the victim are not common characteristics of offenders in the NCVS data. Only about 1 in 4 offenders used a weapon against victims, and 1 in 5 caused injury to victims (Harlow, 2005; Masucci & Langton, 2017). Substance use might be assumed to be a contributing factor for offenders committing crimes of hate, but data show that this is not common. Offenders were perceived by victims to be under the influence of alcohol or drugs in about 30% of the hate crime victimization reported in the NCVS (Harlow, 2005; Langton & Planty, 2011).

Summary

In this chapter, we have given an overview of the patterns and trends for hate crime. The volume of total hate crimes in America was addressed showing the difference between data collection programs and units of analysis. Information on bias motivation was provided to show patterns by category and specific type, illustrating which categories of bias occur more often and which targeted groups experience more hate crime. Patterns for offense types explained that most hate crimes involve vandalism, intimidation, simple or aggravated assault. Data from the NCVS were used to display patterns for victim and offender characteristics. The information provided should provide a better understand of the nature and occurrence of hate crime.

References

Federal Bureau of Investigation. (1993). *Hate crimes statistics, 1992.* https://www.ncjrs.gov/pdf-files1/Digitization/149507NCJRS.pdf.

Federal Bureau of Investigation. (1994–2019). *Hate crime statistics, annual reports.* https://www.fbi.gov/services/cjis/ucr/publications#Hate-Crime%20Statistics.

Federal Bureau of Investigation. (2019a). Hate crime statistics, 2018. https://ucr.fbi.gov/hate-crime/2018.

Federal Bureau of Investigation. (2019b). *Hate crime statistics, 2018: Offenders.* https://ucr.fbi.gov/hate-crime/2018/topic-pages/offenders.

Federal Bureau of Investigation. (2019c). *Crime in the United States, 2018: Offense definitions.* https://ucr.fbi.gov/crime-in-the-u.s/2018/crime-in-the-u.s.-2018/topic-pages/offense-definitions.

Federal Bureau of Investigation. (2019d). *Summary of NIBRS, 2018.* https://ucr.fbi.gov/nibrs/2018/resource-pages/summary.pdf.

Federal Bureau of Investigation. (2012). *Hate crime statistics, 2011.* https://ucr.fbi.gov/hate-crime/2011.

Federal Bureau of Investigation. (2013). *Hate crime statistics, 2012.* https://ucr.fbi.gov/hate-crime/2012.

Federal Bureau of Investigation. (2014). *Hate crime statistics, 2013.* https://ucr.fbi.gov/hate-crime/2013.

Federal Bureau of Investigation. (2015). *Hate crime statistics, 2014.* https://ucr.fbi.gov/hate-crime/2014.

Federal Bureau of Investigation. (2016). *Hate crime statistics, 2015.* https://ucr.fbi.gov/hate-crime/2015.

Federal Bureau of Investigation. (2017). *Hate crime statistics, 2016.* https://ucr.fbi.gov/hate-crime/2016.

Federal Bureau of Investigation. (2018). *Hate crime statistics, 2017.* https://ucr.fbi.gov/hate-crime/2017.

Harlow, C. W. (2005). *Hate crime reported by victims and police.* Washington, DC: US Department of Justice, Office of Justice Programs, Bureau of Justice Statistics.

Langton, L., & Planty, M. (2011). *Hate crime, 2003–2009.* Washington, DC: US Department of Justice, Office of Justice Programs, Bureau of Justice Statistics.

Masucci, M., & Langton, L. (2017). *Hate crime victimization, 2004–2015.* Washington, DC: US Department of Justice Office of Justice Programs Bureau of Justice Statistics.

Sandholtz, N., Langton, L., & Planty, M. (2013). *Hate crime victimization, 2003–2011.* Washington, DC: US Department of Justice, Office of Justice Programs, Bureau of Justice Statistics.

Wilson, M. M. (2014). *Hate crime victimization, 2004–2012: Statistical tables.* Washington, DC: US Department of Justice, Office of Justice Programs, Bureau of Justice Statistics.

Chapter 6
The Uniqueness of Hate Crimes

Abstract This chapter examines the rational that supports penalty enhancing statutes and sanctions for hate motivated violence. To this end, the chapter delves into theories and studies that posit hate crimes are uniquely different than their ordinary crime counterparts. The chapter reviews empirical evidence that has found physical, psychological, and quality of life coping differences that reflect the severity of injuries to hate crime victims. In addition, the impact of victims possessing immutable characteristics and the inability to use victim blaming techniques to avoid future victimizations is discussed. Chapter 6 also includes a discussion of possible intervening factors that research has uncovered that likely exacerbate the severity of bias victim injuries. The chapter includes a discussion of vicarious victimization effects on secondary victims and illuminates the effectiveness of the messages that hate crime offenders send to all members of their target bias victim groups. Lastly, chapter 6 examines the differential impact of the hate crime experience on racial and ethnic minorities.

Keywords Hate crime injuries · Bias motivated injuries · Co-offending injuries · Physical injuries · Psychological injuries · Quality of life coping injuries · In terrorum effects · Immutable characteristics · Victim blaming techniques

This chapter focuses on the unique characteristics of hate crimes and reviews theories and studies that sought to distinguish the harm of bias from non-bias motivated offending. The idea that 45 states and the District of Columbia have enacted penalty enhancement provisions in their hate crime statutes (ADL, 2019) reflects a general consensus that hate crimes hurt more, and consequently, should be punished more. Hate crime scholars and advocates have theorized and demonstrated through research that hate crime is quite unique in its consequences to victims (Iganski, 2001; Levin & McDevitt, 1993). However, opponents of hate crime statutes argue constitutional and practical problems with hate crime legislation should negate legislative remedies applied through penalty enhancement sanctions.

© The Author(s), under exclusive license to Springer Nature Switzerland
AG 2021
F. S. Pezzella, M. D. Fetzer, *The Measurement of Hate Crimes in America*,
SpringerBriefs in Criminology, https://doi.org/10.1007/978-3-030-51577-5_6

The fundamental premise of sanctioning hate crimes more severely than ordinary crimes is based on the notion that the consequential injuries of such crimes are more severe with far reaching ramifications. This rationale is reflected in the legislative notes of hate crime statutes such as 18 U.S. § 249 and in the decision regarding Wisconsin v. Mitchell (1993). In *Mitchell*, the Court supported the state of Wisconsin's argument that proscribing enhanced punishment for hate crimes was a compelling state interest because of the possibility of retaliatory victimization and the detrimental impact on society at large. Hate crimes have also been found to exact more severe injuries on victims relative to their non-bias crime counterparts (Messner, McHugh, & Felson, 2004; Pezzella & Fetzer, 2017). Finally, hate crimes, unlike their non-bias crime counterparts, have a distinct negative effect on secondary victims (Lim, 2009; Perry & Alvi, 2012). Secondary victims are those who share group membership with the primary victim but was not the direct target of the offender. Lawrence (1999) explained how and why hate crimes are different. He asserted that true hate crimes reflect a mental state of the offender to do harm to a victim based on animus for a particular group of which the victim is a member. Thus, culpability is based on the state of mind of the offender to perpetrate prejudicial harm. Unlike ordinary crime victimizations, hate crime victimizations are impersonal. That is, victims are targeted for what they represent, having nothing at all to do with any of the individual qualities of the victim and everything to do with the victim's group membership. To this extent, both Lawrence (1999) and Mason (2015) suggest that the hate crime offender's moral culpability is greater than that of similar offenders whose conduct lacks the element of prejudice.

Arguably, unlike ordinary crimes, the victim's inability to minimize further risk because of immutable characteristics makes hate crime victimization that much more injurious. Neither primary or secondary victims can escape vulnerability because of personal characteristics that cannot be changed. Levin (2002) argued that hate crimes are unlike parallel ordinary crimes because they are serial in nature and tend to extend to secondary victimizations or retaliatory hate crimes. As a result, he argued governments have a compelling interest in promulgating legislation that severely punishes hate crime offending. Finally, several scholars have noted that hate crimes are unique because they are multidimensional and exact severe physical and psychological injuries on primary and secondary victims and on society at large. (Iganski, 2001; Lawrence, 1999; Perry, 2015; Perry & Alvi, 2012; Pezzella & Fetzer, 2017).

Physical Injuries

Hate crime scholars have advanced quite a few theories and empirical investigations over the last few decades to distinguish the severity of physical injuries of hate crimes from those of ordinary crimes. For example, Herek, Gillis, and Cogan (1999) and Lawrence (1999) suggest the physical injuries of hate crimes can be distinguished by the relative increase in symptomology of bias crime victims. One of the earliest claims about the relationship between hate crime victimizations and sever-ity of injuries was presented by Levin and McDevitt (1993). Their review of Boston police department records found that 50% of hate crimes involved severe injuries that required hospitalization. Their findings were supported by Strom's (2001) National Incident-Based Reporting System (NIBRS) analysis of aggravated assaults between 1997 and 1999. He found that sixty percent of the total bias crimes studied involved serious injury. McDevitt, Balboni, Garcia, and Gu (2001) also found dif-ferences in the severity of injuries between bias and non-bias victims in a study of 452 aggravated assaults in Boston from 1992 to 1997. They reported the "exces-sively brutal" nature of hate crimes that required hospitalization far exceeded paral-lel non-bias crimes. These findings were supported by Levin's (2002) premise that hate crimes were twice as likely to cause injury and four times more likely to cause hospitalization.

In another empirical investigation, Messner et al. (2004) used a 1999 NIBRS sample that included situational, offender, and victim data to analyze cases involv-ing intimidation, simple, and aggravated assaults. With respect to comparative inju-ries, they found that racial and other bias-motivated assaults were three times more likely to result in major injuries including broken bones and severe lacerations. They also found that hate crimes primarily involved multiple offenders who were more likely to be strangers and use alcohol and illegal drugs which contributed to the severity of injuries that victims sustained. In addition, they reported African Americans and other ethnic minorities were more likely to be victims of bias crimes than Whites.

Pezzella and Fetzer (2017) used a 2010 NIBRS sample to assess differences in physical injuries associated with bias and non-bias aggravated assaults. They hypothesized that bias crimes were more likely to result in serious physical injury than non-bias crimes, and that specific types of bias were more likely to result in serious physical injury than non-bias types. Consistent with Messner et al. (2004) investigation, they found demographic factors unique to the bias experience. Victims of bias assaultive crimes were more likely to be minority and male. Criminal bias incidents were more likely committed by strangers in the company of multiple offenders, who used alcohol and drugs which contributed to the seriousness of inju-ries. Interestingly, Pezzella and Fetzer (2017) found no significant differences in the likelihood of serious injuries between bias compared to non-bias assaults in the general bias categories of race, ethnicity, sexual orientation, religion, and disability. However, when the bias categories were disaggregated into bias types, only victims of anti-White and anti-Lesbian hate crimes were significantly more likely to experi-ence serious injuries. In a subsequent study, Fetzer and Pezzella (2019) used more a representative sample derived from the 2013 National Crime Victimization Survey (NCVS). They hypothesized that bias crime victims, in comparison with non-bias crime victims, sustain more severe physical and psychological injuries. Physical injuries were classified into three categories: no injuries, minor, and serious injuries. Covariates introduced in the study based on previous research included whether the crimes were bias-motivated; if a firearm, knife, other or unknown weapon was involved; and whether the incident included multiple offenders, drug and alcohol use, or involved a stranger. They found that bias assaults were 23% more likely to result in a serious physical injury and weapons substantially increased the odds of serious injury. Moreover, the existence of multiple offenders or drug and alcohol use increased the likelihood of serious injury. Their findings supported the notion that bias crime victimizations are more physically injurious than their non-bias crimes.

In two other investigations of the physical injuries, researchers affirmed that bias crime victimization was more likely to result in relatively severe physical injuries but also found that the relationship was more nuanced than delineated by previous research. Drawing from previous research on interracial crime, Powers and Socia (2019) tested the theories of adversary effect, racial threat, and racial animosity to explain offending patterns and injury severity. The overall purpose of the study was to examine whether the race of the victim and offender, considered in tandem with racial bias, affected the likelihood of serious injury. Contrary to previous theories of greater likelihood of Black victims suffering serious injuries, they found that Black on White victims of hate crimes represented the highest chance of sustaining either minor or major injuries and White on Black victims of hate crimes reflected the lowest chance of incurring either injuries. Refuting previous theories of bias motivated animus as an explanation for White on Black hate crimes, they asserted "the findings of this study correspond to some previous research that found Black offenders more likely to injure their victims compared to white offenders." (Powers & Socia, 2019, p. 465) They also posited "we cannot assume racial animosity as a framework to situate interracial violence" (p. 465). Powers and Socia's (2019) research supported previous theories that found a relationship between bias-motivated offending and severity of injury. However, their findings indicated that the direction of the victimization severity is opposite of the findings proclaimed in previous hate crime scholarship.

Another recent study of bias-motivated crime and the severity of injury used the NCVS. Tessler, Langton, Rivara, Vavilala, and Rowhani-Rahbar (2018) examined 13 years (2004–2013) of data to determine the risks and health impacts of race- and ethnicity-motivated violent victimization. Their study addressed three research questions relevant to offender and victim race/ethnicity-motivated violent crimes: (1) Are Non-Hispanic Black and Hispanic individuals at greater risk for race/ethnicity-motivated violent crime compared to Whites?; (2) Are race/ethnicity-motivated violent crimes more severe for Non-Hispanic Black and Hispanic victims juxtaposed to Non-Hispanic Whites?; and (3) Longitudinally, what trends are suggested by examining annual rates of victimization from race/ethnicity bias, other bias, and non-bias by victim race/ethnicity? They found 30% higher risk of race/ethnicity bias-motivated violent victimization for non-Hispanic Blacks and Hispanics compared to Non-Hispanic Whites. Moreover, they found more frequent and serious violent crime, involving weapons and firearms and more injuries and victimizations involving medical care for non-Hispanic Black and Hispanic victims. They reported that "while race and ethnicity–motivated bias crimes are decreasing for Non-Hispanic Whites and Hispanics, the trend for Non-Hispanic Blacks since 2010 has been slowly increasing" (Tessler et al., 2018 p. 11).

The last study we reviewed detected an intervening factor in the relationship between bias-motivated victimization and severity of physical injury. Lantz and Kim's (2019) NIBRS analysis found that bias-motivated incidents in comparison to non-bias incidents are more likely to result in serious injuries. However, bias-motivated crimes are more likely to involve co-offending that exacerbate serious injuries.

Psychological Injuries

In addition to being more physically injurious, hate crimes have also been thought to be more detrimental because they negatively impact the core identity of the victim (Lawrence, 1999; Perry & Alvi, 2012). Some scholars compare the emotional and psychological injuries of hate crimes with the trauma characteristics of rape victims (Lawrence, 1999; Lim, 2009). Studies that have examined victims in the aftermath of the hate crime incident have found an array of psychological symptoms that support Iganski's (2001) proposition that hate crime hurt more (Berrill, 1990; Herek et al., 1999). Some of the earliest studies of the psychological and emotional injuries in the aftermath of hate crime victimization were conducted with lesbian, gay, or bisexual (LGB) victims of anti-sexual orientation hate crimes. These studies have found that psychological and emotional injuries in the aftermath of the hate crime incident are quite traumatic with most finding that victims are fearful of future victimization. For instance, Berrill (1990) conducted one of the earliest anti-gay violence studies thirty years ago. He reported that lesbian, gay, and bi-sexual victims (LGB) not only feared harassment and violence, but also anticipated future victimizations. Similarly, Herek et al. (1999) studied behavioral and psychological injuries resulting from LGB bias victimizations nearly a decade later. Utilizing a snowball sample, they compiled 2,259 victims including 1,170 women and 1,089 men. Their findings were consistent with Berrill's (1990). Compared to non-bias crime victims, bias crime victims sustained more fear of crime, greater perceived vulnerability, and lower self-mastery of personal outcomes. In addition, they reported that LGB bias victims experienced more depressive, traumatic symptoms, and feelings of vulnerability and powerlessness regarding their sexual orientation and personal identity in the victimization aftermath. They concluded that LGB victims endure distinct adverse psychological sequelae nearly five years after their experience with the hate crime incident. Herek, Cogan, and Gillis' (2002) analysis of a convenience sample of 450 LGB victims a few years later affirmed their original findings. LGB victims again experienced higher levels of fear and psychological stress relative to non-bias victims during the same period. Craig-Henderson and Sloan (2003) also reported similar findings asserting that even when bias crime victims are able to resume normal activities, "they report living in extreme fear of both their attackers who are rarely apprehended, and those they do not know who resemble their attackers" (p. 483). The psychological injuries of anti-LGB hate crimes in the aftermath of victimization was also detected by Dragowski, Halkitis,

Grossman, and D'Augelli (2011) who surveyed LGB youth victims about their life experiences. They reported that LGB youth victims exhibited symptoms of post-traumatic stress related to verbal and physical anti-sexual orientation victimizations and homophobia.

Several researchers examined psychological and emotional injuries on more diverse samples of bias crime victims and also detected significant psychological and emotionally traumatic injuries. Ehrlich, Ehrlich, Larcom, and Purvis (1994) surveyed a nationally representative sample of respondents and classified them into four groups including non-victims, group defamation, personal, and bias crime victims. Among the four groups of victims, bias crime victims experienced the greatest mean number of psychophysiological symptoms and behavioral variations on a scale of 19 symptoms of posttraumatic stress and 12 social behavioral changes. The researchers reported that bias crime victims experienced significantly greater trauma than do victims of violence committed for other reasons. They concluded severe and important psychophysiological injuries differentiated the group affected by hate crimes from the other three groups. Similarly, Garofalo (1997) conducted a telephone survey on the occurrences of hate crimes in New York City between 1987 and 1988 and in the county of Baltimore between 1982 and 1988. The study compared the effects of hate crimes on 30 victims against the effects of non-hate motivated crimes on 28 victims. The author noted distinct differences between the two types of victims. Hate crime victims were more likely to rate their victimization as "very serious" and reported "being very upset" and "frightened" after the incident and more likely to assert the incident had a "great deal" of effect on their lives both in the short term and long term.

In a sample derived from Boston police department records between the years of 1992 and 1997, McDevitt et al. (2001) compared psychological and behavioral injuries for 91 bias and 45 non-bias victims of assault. To evaluate psychological and behavioral injuries, the researchers incorporated the Horowitz impact of events scale to examine post event stress levels of the total sample of victims. Two major psychological themes were detected that distinguished the bias from non-bias victims of assault. Bias victims demonstrated higher mean-level symptoms of intrusiveness and avoidance compared to the non-bias victims of assault. They found that bias crime victims had more difficulty coping with their victimization, were more depressed, feared more crime, felt less safe, and conjured more intrusive thoughts than non-bias crime assault victims.

Research evidence that support findings of differences in the psychological impact of the bias experience in comparison to the non-bias crime experience was also detected in larger, more representative samples. Corcoran, Lader, and Smith (2015) used sample data from the 2012–2014 Crime Survey of England and Wales (CSEW) to assess the experiences of bias and non-bias victims of crime. They assessed whether CSEW survey respondents had an emotional reaction after the bias incident. For respondents that reported in the affirmative, they were subsequently asked how much and in what ways they were affected. Of the CSEW survey respondents who reported they were emotionally affected, victims of hate crimes were more affected than otherwise-motivated victims. Consistent with previous findings of psychological trauma (Herek et al., 1999, 2002; McDevitt et al., 2001), more than twice as many hate crime victims reported they had suffered a loss of confidence or felt vulnerable after the incident, compared with otherwise-motivated crime victims. Hate crime victims were also more likely to experience fear, difficultly sleeping, anxiety or panic attacks, and depression.

Finally, recall Fetzer and Pezzella (2019) analyzed physical and psychological victimization effects on bias crime victims in their study of NCVS data. They found that when assaults were motivated by hate, the odds of victims suffering psychological trauma were 150% greater than when attacks were not motivated by bias. When offenders used a firearm or knife the odds of psychological trauma significantly increased by 5% and 2% respectively. Interestingly, the odds of experiencing psychological trauma was 80% greater when the offender was under the influence of alcohol or drugs.

Differential Impact of the Hate Crime Experience on Racial and Ethnic Minorities

It is pretty much widely known that racial and ethnic minorities are the most prevalent victims of hate crimes (Messner et al., 2004; Pezzella & Fetzer, 2017; Tessler et al., 2018). However, several scholars also postulate that hate crimes against historically victimized groups inflict a unique psychological harm in and of itself (Craig-Henderson & Sloan, 2003; Lawrence, 1999). Lawrence (1999) posited that bias crimes against racial minorities are uniquely injurious because the basic purpose of the offender is to triggers the history and social context of prejudice and violence against the victim and his group. Craig-Henderson and Sloan (2003) posited the following concern about racist hate crimes perpetrated against African Americans:

> For people of color, and in particular African Americans, racist hate crimes have a regrettably long history. These incidents born of racism, have occurred within a cultural context that has consistently jeopardized the physical and psychological well-being of African Americans and others. Indeed, the effects of racism has been so profound that contemporary health psychologists agree that any comprehensive model of minority health must take account the way race impacts health status. When an anti-Black racist hate crime occurs, it brings all of the dormant feelings of anger, fear and pain to the collective psychological forefront of the victim. This is not the case when White are targets of racist hate crimes and though the consequences of such victimization is likely to be traumatic for the targeted individual, the incident is not likely to engender despair or anger among all other whites who learn of the incident (p. 485).

Helms, Nicolas, and Green (2012) also discussed the uniqueness of injuries resulting from hate crimes noting the conspicuous absence in contemporary trauma literature of treatment modalities for racism and hate crime and their catalytic effects on post-traumatic stress syndrome (PTSD). They found that researchers fail to view hate crime victim experiences as particularly detrimental because the historical roots of the trauma are invisible to them. They suggessted that hate incidents may arouse PTSD and related symptoms in victims as a consequence of recalling memories or identity group histories that threaten life or psychological integrity.

These scholars suggest that the psychological and emotional harm to certain victimized groups may be more severe than harm to other groups who do not share a history of hate crime victimization. Individual victims that are members of groups that have been historically targeted for violence likely experience excessive psychological trauma consistent with the intent of the offenders.

Behavioral and Coping Injuries

One of the major impacts of the bias victimization experience is the quality of life changes that victims tend to undergo post victimization. Studies of victim behavior in the aftermath of crime incidents informs us that victims naturally change their routines in order to minimize the chances of future victimization. However, hate crime victimizations are unlike ordinary crime victimizations. Recall, Lawrence (1999) noted that bias victims, unlike non-bias victim, are targeted not for *who* they are, but for *what* they are. Consequently, the behavioral modifications and changes in routines for bias victims are arguably more dramatic and life changing because the immutable characteristics the victims possess. In most victimization experiences, victims are able to examine themselves and modify what they perceived to have increased their risk of being victimized (McDevitt et al., 2001). McDevitt et al. (2001) explain this defensive maneuver as victim blaming. It allows the victim some degree of psychological and emotional security to understand that they have acted in a way to buffer themselves against future victimization. Because of immutable characteristics, hate crime victims are unable to utilize victim blaming techniques to avoid repeat victimization. Consequently, the victimization experience bears heavily on the quality of life of hate crime victims. Extreme life changing behaviors and coping strategies include changing jobs or relocating to regain some sense of personal safety in their daily life routines (Craig-Henderson & Sloan, 2003). Iganski and Lagou (2015) reported behavioral injuries in their analysis of severity and types of injuries sustained in bias and otherwise motivated crime victims. Comparing household and bias crime victims, they found bias victims were more likely to report avoidance measures including avoiding walking and going certain places, moving away, trying to be more alert, and not so trusting.

Secondary Victimizations

Another reason hate crimes are purported to be uniquely more injurious that otherwise motivated crimes is because of the deleterious effects on secondary victims and on society at large (Gerstenfeld, 2018; Iganski, 2001: Lawrence, 1999;

Weinstein, 1992. Hate crimes are generally conceived as messages to primary victims, and distal members of the victim's group, that they are of marginal value (Fetzer & Pezzella, 2020; Lawrence, 1999). Moreover, members of the target community of a bias crime perceive the crime as an attack on themselves directly and individually (Lawrence, 1999; Manzi & Dunn, 2007). The primary victim may be selected as the target of hate, but the message is clear and apparent to all the members in the victim's subgroup (Lim, 2009). Perry's (2001) definition of hate crimes reflects the mental state and purpose of the hate offender's efforts to target secondary victims:

> It is an act of violence and intimidation, usually directed towards already stigmatized and marginalized groups. As such, it is a mechanism of power, intended to reaffirm the precarious hierarchies that characterize a given social order. It attempts to recreate simultaneously the threatened (real or imagined) hegemony of the perpetrators group and the appropriate subordinate identity of the victim's group (p. 10).

McDevitt et al. (2001) noted the interchangeable dimension of hate crime victimization. That is, any potential victim within the targeted group will suffice for the offender. Random persons that happen to share immutable characteristics with the primary victim are vulnerable because of the unique interchangeable aspect of hate crimes victims. Consequently, hate crimes perpetrated against primary victims retain the capacity to create psychological trauma in secondary victims. Chakraborti and Garland (2015) described "hate crimes as classic stranger danger crimes that are designed to send an intimidating message not just to the individual, but to other members of that group" (p. 107). The effect of secondary victimization was not lost to Iganski and Lagou (2015) who asserted hate crimes have an impact on the spatial mobility of victimized communities. Vicarious victims create mental maps of where to not go. Consequently, the spatial mobility of all members perceived to share characteristics with the primary victims becomes restricted. Much like the restrictive behavior and coping measures taken by primary victims, the everyday behaviors of secondary victims including shopping and going to work are also disrupted and access to public facilities potentially curtailed.

There is very scant empirical research on vicarious victimizations and the studies that are available incorporate small, perhaps, non-generalizable samples. Still the findings support theories that posit hate crimes perpetrate secondary victimizations. Lim (2009), relying on a snowball methodology, conducted a content analysis of 45 Asian Americans between 2002 and 2003 about their experiences with racial bigotry and hate crime. A common theme throughout the 45 interviews was the pervasive role of white males as offenders who wished to express their superiority and instill the notion that Asian Americans were perpetual non-white foreigners who did not belong. Lim (2009) asserted the narratives "overwhelming reflected the views of Asian Americans on how they perceive and experience hate crimes committed by the White majority" (p. 108). Lim (2009) described a pattern of responses that explicitly demonstrated how the harm of hate extended beyond the direct victims to the targeted populations. Lim (2009) asserted that "hate violence permeated the minds of his subjects and was always anticipated and carefully managed" (p. 119).

He described hate crimes as message crimes that terrorize populations because perpetrators view victims as interchangeable symbols. Lastly, he described hate crimes are symbolic crimes designed to send terror messages to targeted communities.

Perry and Alvi (2012) attempted to assess the experiences of a larger secondary victim sample utilizing respondent driven sampling methodology to attain study subjects. Although their survey received very few responses, they assessed the survey responses they did receive and compiled themes from focus group meetings. Based on the limited number of surveys returned and the focus group discussions, the researchers conceptualized the injuries to secondary victims as "in terrorum" effects. They described five injurious effects of hate crimes on secondary victims. First, victims were shocked and disappointed that hate crimes still exist in our age and community. Second, victims garnered anger and both specific and generalized outrage towards perpetrators and a culture of bias and exclusion. Third, victims developed fear and a sense of vulnerability and understood the hate message that offenders wish to send. Fourth, the offender's perception of inferiority and subordination of victims and their communities was affirmed. Finally, victims accepted the idea that hate crime in association with its stigmatization and marginalization is normative. Concern about the severity of secondary victimizations was also indicated in the legislative findings supporting the passage of 18 U.S. § 249. "A prominent characteristic of a violent crime motivated by bias is that it devastates not just the actual victim and the family and friends of the victim, but frequently savages the community sharing the traits that caused the victim to be selected." (p. 3) Secondary victimizations represent another unique dimension of bias motivated crime.

Injuries to Society at Large

Hate crimes are also thought to have a detrimental impact on society at large. In an age of inclusiveness and diversity, many governments enact legislation that support the ideals of equality, shared values and goals. Scholars assert that hate crimes create and or exacerbate intergroup suspicion and distrust and undermine collective efficacy (Perry, 2015). Perry (2015) asserted that if hate crimes in society are left unchallenged and allowed to perpetuate, relationships within communities will deteriorate along with societal goals of inclusion, equity, and equal justice. Other hate crime scholars and practitioners expressed the same concern. Weinstein (1992) asserted racial violence has particularly pernicious ramifications for society as a whole. Iganski (2001) posited one of the five levels of harm of hate crimes is to "societal values and norms" (p. 29). The Supreme Court in deciding on the legality of penalty enhancing statutes in *Wisconsin v. Mitchell* agreed with the state and its amici that bias-motivated crimes are more likely to provoke retaliatory crimes, inflict emotional harm on its victims, and incite community unrest. Concerns about the impact on society at large was also expressed in support of the enactment of 18 U.S. the Matthew Shepard and James Byrd Jr. Hate Crime Prevention Act AND include a section sign after US and 249 with the congressional finding that "such violence disrupts the tranquility and safety of communities and is deeply divisive." (p. 3)

Summary

This chapter reviewed studies that found hate crimes quite unique. Researchers found hate crime are more likely to be perpetrated by strangers and multiple offenders when under the influence of alcohol or drugs contributes toward severe injuries (Messner et al., 2004; Pezzella & Fetzer, 2017). In addition, the studies reviewed in this chapter reported that bias victimizations are likely to sustain serious physical, psychological, emotional, and behavioral quality of life injuries compared to their non-bias crime counterparts (Corcoran et al., 2015; Ehrlich et al., 1994; Fetzer & Pezzella, 2019; Herek et al., 1999; McDevitt et al., 2001). The research assessed in this chapter also noted findings that the likelihood of injuries was more nuco-offending injuriesanced than previously reported. Empirical investigations that found mixed findings were reported that alternately found that Black or White victims were more likely to be severely injured (Pezzella & Fetzer, 2017; Powers & Socia, 2019) and that co-offending intervened significantly in the seriousness of injury to bias victims (Lantz & Kim, 2019). Lastly, several researchers discussed the deleterious impact of hate crimes on secondary victims and on society at large contending that this type of offending supports the notion that hate crime are unique because they hurt more (Iganski, 2001; Lim, 2009; Perry & Alvi, 2012; Weinstein, 1992).

References

Anti-Defamation League. (2019) *Anti-defamation league state hate crime statutory provisions.* http:// www.adl.org/
Berrill, K. T. (1990). Anti-gay violence and victimization in the United States: An overview. *Journal of Interpersonal Violence, 5*(3), 274–294.
Chakraborti, N., & Garland, J. (2015). *Hate crime: Impact, causes and responses.* Los Angeles: Sage Publications.
Corcoran, H., Lader, D., & Smith, K. (2015). Hate crime, England and Wales. *Statistical Bulletin, 5,* 15.
Craig-Henderson, K., & Sloan, L. R. (2003). After the hate: Helping psychologists help victims of racist hate crime. *Clinical Psychology: Science and Practice, 10*(4), 481–490.
Dragowski, E. A., Halkitis, P. N., Grossman, A. H., & D'Augelli, A. R. (2011). Sexual orientation victimization and posttraumatic stress symptoms among lesbian, gay, and bisexual youth. *Journal of Gay & Lesbian Social Services, 23*(2), 226–249.
Ehrlich, H., Ehrlich, H., Larcom, B., & Purvis, R. (1994). The traumatic effects of ethnoviolence. *Hate and Bias Crime: A Reader,* 153–167.
Fetzer, M. D., & Pezzella, F. S. (2019). The nature of bias crime injuries: A comparative analysis of physical and psychological victimization effects. *Journal of Interpersonal Violence, 34*(18), 3864–3887.
Fetzer, M. D., & Pezzella, F. S. (2020). Hate crimes: A special category of victimization. In R. Geffner, V. Vieth, V. Naughan-Eden, A. Rosenbaum, L. Hamberger, & J. White (Eds.), *Handbook of interpersonal violence across the lifespan.* Springer.
Garofalo, J. (1997). Hate crime victimization in the United State. In R. C. Davis, A. J. Lurigio, & W. G. Skogan (Eds.), *Victims of crime* (pp. 134–145). Thousand Oaks, CA: Sage publications.

Gerstenfeld, P. B. (2018). *Hate crimes: Causes, controls and controversies*. Thousand Oaks: Sage.

Helms, J. E., Nicolas, G., & Green, C. E. (2012). Racism and ethnoviolence as trauma: Enhancing professional training. *Traumatology, 16*(4), 53–62.

Herek, G. M., Cogan, J. C., & Gillis, J. R. (2002). Victim experiences in hate crimes based on sexual orientation. *Journal of Social Issues, 58*(2), 319–339.

Herek, G. M., Gillis, J. R., & Cogan, J. C. (1999). Psychological sequelae of hate-crime victimization among lesbian, gay, and bisexual adults. *Journal of Consulting and Clinical Psychology, 67*(6), 945.

Iganski, P. (2001). Hate crimes hurt more. *American Behavioral Scientist, 45*(4), 626–638.

Iganski, P., & Lagou, S. (2015). The personal injuries of 'hate crime'. In *The Routledge international handbook on hate crime* (pp. 52–64). London: Routledge.

Lantz, B., & Kim, J. (2019). Hate crimes hurt more, but so do co-offenders: Separating the influence of co-offending and bias on hate-motivated physical injury. *Criminal Justice and Behavior, 46*(3), 437–456.

Lawrence, F. M. (1999). *Punishing hate*. Harvard University Press.

Levin, B. (2002). From slavery to hate crime laws: The emergence of race and status-based protection in American criminal law. *Journal of Social Issues, 58*(2), 227–245.

Levin, J., & McDevitt, J. (1993). *Hate crimes: The rising tide of bigotry and bloodshed*. New York, NY: Springer.

Lim, H. A. (2009). Beyond the immediate victim: Understanding hate crimes as message crimes. *Hate Crimes: The Consequences of Hate Crime, 2*, 107–222.

Manzi, & Dunn. (2007). Hate crime victimization: A legal perspective. In L. J. Moriarty & R. A. Jerin (Eds.), *Current issues in victimology research*. Carolina Academic Press.

Mason, G. (2015). Legislating against hate. In *The Routledge international handbook on hate crime* (pp. 77–86). Routledge.

McDevitt, J., Balboni, J., Garcia, L., & Gu, J. (2001). Consequences for victims: A comparison of bias-and non-bias-motivated assaults. *American Behavioral Scientist, 45*(4), 697–713.

Messner, S. F., McHugh, S., & Felson, R. B. (2004). Distinctive characteristics of assaults motivated by bias. *Criminology, 42*(3), 585–618.

Perry, B. (2001). *In the name of hate: Understanding hate crimes*. Psychology Press.

Perry, B. (2015). Exploring the community impacts of hate crime. In *The Routledge international handbook on hate crime* (pp. 65–76). Routledge.

Perry, B., & Alvi, S. (2012). 'We are all vulnerable': The in terrorem effects of hate crimes. *International Review of Victimology, 18*(1), 57–71.

Pezzella, F. S., & Fetzer, M. D. (2017). The likelihood of injury among bias crimes: An analysis of general and specific bias types. *Journal of Interpersonal Violence, 32*(5), 703–729.

Powers, R. A., & Socia, K. M. (2019). Racial animosity, adversary effect, and hate crime: Parsing out injuries in intraracial, interracial, and race-based offenses. *Crime & Delinquency, 65*(4), 447–473.

Strom, K. (2001). *Hate crimes reported in NIBRS, 1997–99*. Washington, DC: US Department of Justice, Office of Justice Programs, Bureau of Justice Statistics.

Tessler, R. A., Langton, L., Rivara, F. P., Vavilala, M. S., & Rowhani-Rahbar, A. (2018). Differences by victim race and ethnicity in race-and ethnicity-motivated violent bias crimes: A national study. *Journal of Interpersonal Violence*. https://doi.org/10.1177/0886260518818428

The Matthew Shepard and James Byrd Jr. Hate crime Prevention Act 18 U.S. § 249

Weinstein, J. (1992). *First amendment challenges to hate crime legislation: Where's the speech?*

Wisconsin v. Mitchell. (1993) *U.S. Supreme Court, 505 U.S. 476.*

Chapter 7
Victim Underreporting

Abstract This chapter looks at the issues of victim underreporting and its consequences for inaccurate measurement of hate crimes. The chapter reviews the differences in reports of hate crime by the two major sources of official hate crime data,
the FBIs Uniform Crime Report Hate Crime Statistics program and the Bureau of
Justice Statistics National Crime Victimization Survey (NVCS). Chapter 7 explores
bias victim's groups that are likely to underreport and some of the reasons they may
not report. Specifically, the chapter focuses on the dark figure of hate crime underreporting examining the reasons victims themselves asserted as reasons for not
reporting in their responses to the NCVS. Chapter 7 also delves into the relationship
between victim's perception of police legitimacy and the likelihood of reporting.
Finally, the chapter also compares reporting practices of hate crime victims to ordinary crime victims highlighting similarities and differences.

Keywords Victim underreporting · Bias victim groups not likely to report · Dark
figure of hate crime underreporting · Police legitimacy and hate crime reporting ·
Reason for not reporting hate crimes

Victim underreporting is one of the largest obstacles to measuring the prevalence
and severity of hate crimes. It is widely known that the majority of victims do not
report their victimization. This is quite evident when a comparison is made between
the annual reports of police recorded hate crimes published through the annual
FBI's Uniform Crime Report (UCR) and the National Crime Victimization Survey
(NCVS) reports published by the Bureau of Justice Statistics (BJS). From 2003 to
2015, the average number of hate crimes reported by police was 8370; however, for
this same period 252,630 victimizations per year were reported (Fetzer & Pezzella,
2020; Masucci & Langton, 2017, p. 8). Of the total number of victimizations
reported, Masucci and Langton (2017) indicate that 104,600 were reported to police
of which 14,380 were confirmed by police investigators. We think the disparity in
official reports and the problems of measuring hate crimes is quite clear when these

F. S. Pezzella, M. D. Fetzer, *The Measurement of Hate Crimes in America*,
SpringerBriefs in Criminology, https://doi.org/10.1007/978-3-030-51577-5_7

drastically different accounts of reported hate crimes are examined. Undoubtedly, there is a substantial dark figure of hate crime underreporting (Comey, 2014; Pezzella, Fetzer, & Keller, 2019). The question remains, however, how do we reconcile these vastly divergent numbers between the UCR and the NCVS. What issues facilitate victim underreporting of hate crime? Who are the victims that do not report and why don't they report their victimization? Research has uncovered a number of reasons why victims do not report hate crimes (Wong & Christmann, 2008) and these reasons likely vary by victim groups (Martin, 1996; Zaykowski, 2010). For instance, the reasons Asian victims may not report may be different than the reasons African Americans victims decide not to report. Likewise, it is quite feasible that the reasons Hispanic victims don't report may be for a different set of reasons than LGBTQ victims elect not to report. This chapter addresses these issues by focusing on the reasons bias victim groups decide not to report their victimizations. We surmise that if the impediments to victim underreporting can be removed, a proportional improvement in estimates of hate crime prevalence will result.

Bias Victims Least Likely to Report

To understand the significance of bias crime victim underreporting, it is useful to assess the most prevalent reasons why they don't report. Using the NCVS, Masucci and Langton (2017) analyzed the reasons why bias crime victimizations were not reported to police. They found that 41% of total hate crime victims and 44% of violent hate victims explained that they handled the matter in another way. Next, 19% of total hate crime victims and 20% of violent hate crime victims reported the incident was "not important enough" to police. Last, 17.5% of total hate crime victims and 15.5% of violent hate crime victims indicated "police would not help" as their reasons for not reporting.

In a recent NCVS study of the dark figure of hate crime underreporting, Pezzella et al. (2019) hypothesized that bias crime victims relative to non-bias crime victims were less likely to report their victimization to police. Using data from the 2014 NCVS, they found significant differences in underreporting between the two categories of victims. Interestingly, they found the magnitude of underreporting for bias crimes increased in models that incrementally added victim, offender, and situational characteristics. The NCVS findings by both Masucci and Langton (2017) and Pezzella et al. (2019) warrant questions about which bias victim groups do not report.

In order to assess bias victim groups least likely to report, an analysis of the NCVS and the reported average of 252,000 victimizations focusing specifically on the victims who asserted they did not report is likely the optimal source of information about victim underreporting.

To begin, it is important to discuss the process in which hate crime victimizations and incidents occur and ultimately lead to a reporting authority. A few researchers have described the sequential process upon which hate crime victimizations and incidents are reported and recorded. Nolan and Akiyama (1999) enumerated a four-step process:

1. Victims report.
2. Police officers record.
3. Police officers determine and verify hate bias.
4. Police agencies participate in the hate crime program (p. 116).

Balboni and McDevitt (2001) articulated the process in more detail emphasizing the victim's understanding that bias may have been a motivating or aggravating factor critical to the victimization. This is important because although the message from the hate crime offender effectively reaches victims (Lim, 2009; Perry & Alvi, 2012) not all victims may process that they have been a victim of a bias motivated crime (Thorneycroft & Asquith, 2015). Accordingly, Balboni and McDevitt (2001) described a seven-step process upon which victims report hate crimes that are ultimately recorded, counted and estimated towards the overall prevalence of hate crimes:

1. Victim understands that a crime has been committed.
2. Victim recognizes that hate (of the victim's real or perceived minority status or attribute) may be a motivating factor.
3. Victim or another person solicits police enforcement intervention.
4. Victim or another party communicates with law enforcement about motivation of the crime.
5. Law enforcement recognizes the element of hate.
6. Law enforcement documents the element of hate and, as appropriate charges the suspect with civil rights or hate/bias offense.
7. Law enforcement records the incident and submits the information to the Uniform Crime reports, Hate Crime Reporting Unit (p. 6).

Bias Victim Groups Reasons for Underreporting

The issues with victim underreporting begin with the decision to report which may occur at Steps 1 or 2 of the reporting process (Balboni & McDevitt, 2001; Nolan & Akiyama, 1999). Although the empirical research into hate crime reporting is somewhat scant, a few scholars have studied which bias victims do not report and the reasons they decided not to report. For instance, the Bureau of Justice Assistance (BJA) (1997) asserts that cultural mores may preclude hate crime reporting. In many Asian cultures, the status as a hate crime victim incurs a dishonorable stigma that is accompanied by shame to the victim's family. Conceivably, filing a report exacerbates the humiliation. Language barriers may also prevent hate crime reporting (BJA, 1997). In the case of undocumented immigrants, amidst a climate of aggressive ICE tactics, fear of deportation is a huge disincentive to hate crime reporting.

Other reasons for not reporting included victim's fear of retaliation (Wong & Christmann, 2008) and victims not understanding that they have suffered a hate crime victimization (Thorneycroft & Asquith, 2015). This is often the case with disability bias victims. Sin (2013) also found disability bias victims were often dissuaded from reporting particularly when they had a learning disability.

Alternatively, LGBTQ victims of hate crimes may not report for several reasons. First, they fear insensitive police processing; secondly, they are apprehensive about secondary victimizations by law enforcement (Berrill, 1990). Berrill (1990) and Berrill and Herek (1990) reported LGB victims' fears include police indifference to disclosing their private, unconventional sexual orientation to family, friends, and the general public.

Distrust and lack of confidence in law enforcement have also been found to affect the propensity for victims to report in other groups and in otherwise-motivated crimes (Martin, 1996). Consequently, is not surprising that these groups (i.e., African American, Hispanic, and LGBTQ victims) may underreport their victimization. The reticence by victims to report hate crime victimizations to police is consistent with theories of underreporting of ordinary crimes.

Theories and empirical research that have examined ordinary non-bias crimes offer valuable insight into the victim's decision making to report. Although relatively scant, there have been some qualitative and quantitative studies of reporting decision making behavior of hate crime victims. Scholars who have studied victim underreporting of ordinary crimes suggest a link between citizen perceptions of police fairness as arbiters of procedural justice and the inclination for victims to report their victimization. More specifically, these scholars contend that there is a hypothetical connection between citizen belief in the authority of the police and their view towards receiving procedural justice (Tyler, 1990; Tyler & Fagan, 2008). However, research into the relationship between citizen perception of police legitimacy and procedural justice has been found to be somewhat nuanced. Tyler (1990) used a general population survey to study the public's responses about recent contacts with the law, reactions to such contacts, and subsequent behavior. He measured citizens' personal morality as the general sets of beliefs as to how one should act in interaction with law enforcement and conceptualized police legitimacy as citizens' perceptions of whether law enforcement officials rightly have authority over them. Tyler (1990) reported that compliance with the law is contingent upon citizen's perception that police are legitimate and their actions fair and not because they fear punishment. He concluded that citizen perception of the likelihood of receiving procedural fairness influenced their compliance with law enforcement authorities.

Victimology scholars have also proposed another set of interrelated factors likely to influence victims' decisions to report that should be considered when studying hate crime victim underreporting. Fohring (2014) explained the relevance of incident-based reporting because of its focus on basic cost benefit analysis (CBA) as an explanation of the process upon which victims make reporting decisions. CBA theories presume the decision to report crimes is the net sum of the weight of the potential benefits such as the likelihood of the return of lost item minus liabilities such as the loss of time reporting to police. Moreover, the primary CBA factors that impact the reporting decision includes the relationship between the victim and the offender, the value of items lost, and the seriousness of the offense. However, CBA theories of victim reporting have also been criticized because of the assumption that victims can make rational reporting decisions amidst the emotional crisis of a criminal victimization (Fohring, 2014).

Greenberg and Beach (2004) addressed the criticism of the CBA incident-reporting theories by adding affective and social elements to account for the emotional context of victimization. They reported three general processes underlie victims' decisions to report to police including: cognitive processes driven by reward and cost considerations; affective processes under laden by emotional trauma; and social processes determined by victims' consultation with others when deliberating the decision to report their victimization to the police. Explanations about the reasoning behind reporting decisions in ordinary crimes was also derived from an analysis of the 2006/2007 British Crime Survey. According to Nicholas, Kershaw, and Walker (2007) the most common reasons for not reporting ordinary crime was that victims they believed the police would or could not do much about the incident or victims perceived incident to be too trivial or no loss occurred. Further, respondents explained that the incident was a private matter. Inconvenience of reporting was also cited by victims along with police related reasons including dislike or fear or previous bad experiences with police or courts.

Wong and Christmann (2008) assessed whether the reporting practices of hate crime victims was similar to that of reporting crime practices of volume crime described in the 2007 British Crime Survey. Incorporating a small qualitative survey that included five focus groups comprised of total 53 respondents that represented traditionally victimized groups, they reported several factors that influenced victim's decision to report. They found that the decision to report largely depended on the severity and frequency of the incident occurrence. Secondly, if victims feared retaliation, reporting was not likely. Similar to Fohring's (2014) incident-based cost benefit analysis theories of decision making, Wong and Christmann (2008) asserted "victims undertake a cost benefits analysis when considering whether to report an incident, one which acts as a powerful disincentive to anything like full reporting" (p. 1). Interestingly, they concluded that since most hate crimes are non-violent, the likelihood of reporting will remain low.

In another qualitative study, Chakraborti and Hardy (2015) assessed the reporting practices of LGBT victims using a snowball sample methodology in which they derived participants from cafes, bars, forums, and other informal networks. From their sample of 50 study participants, they reported five barriers that impacted whether LGBT victims would report. First, they found that victims normalized victimizations as part and parcel of the LGBT life experience. Secondly, they reported respondents distrusted law enforcement and worried their indifference to their victimization would result in them being "outed" (Berrill, 1990; Berrill & Herek, 1990). Thirdly, respondents perceived the reporting process to be time consuming, confusing, and unlikely to yield a successful outcome. Consequently, participants felt there was little point in reporting to police which resulted in a general sense of apathy about the issue of reporting. Next, they found that participants were gener-

Table 7.1 Reasons for Not Reporting or Reporting Victimizations to Police from the NCVS

Reasons for Not Reporting	Reasons for Reporting
Dealt With Another Way	**To Get Help With Incident**
Reported to another offical (guard, apt. manager, school official, etc.)	Stop or prevent THIS incident from happening
Private or personal matter or took care of it myself or informally; told offender's parent	Needed help after incident due to, ect.
Not Important Enough to Respond	**To Recover Loss**
Minor or unsuccessful crime, small or no loss, recovered property	To recover property
Child offender(s), "kid stuff"	To collect insurance
Not clear it was a crime or that harm was intended	**To get Offender**
Insurance Wouldn't Cover	To prevent further crimes against respondent/respondent's household by this offender
No insurance, loss less than deductible, etc.	To stop this offender from committing other crimes against anyone
Police Couldn't Do Anything	To punish offender
Didn't find out until too late	Catch or find offender -other reason or no reason given
Could not recover or identify property	**To Let Police Know**
Could not find or identify offender, lack of proof	To improve police surveilance of respondent's home, area, ect.
Police Wouldn't Help	Duty to let police know about crime
Police wouldn't think it was important enough, wouldn't want to be bothered or get involved	**Other Reason - Specified**
Police would be inefficient, ineffective (they'd arrive late or not at all, wouldn't do a good job, ect.)	
Police would be biased, would harass/insult respondent, cause repondent trouble, ect.	
Offender was police officer	
Other Reason	
Did not want to get offender in trouble with law	
Was advised not to report to police	
Afaid of reprisal by offender or others	
Did not want to or could not take time - too inconvenient	
Other - Specified	

Note: This table shows the response choices for reasons why a victim did not report or report their victimization from the 2016 NCVS Crime Incident Report (BJS, 2016b, pp. 25–26)

ally unaware of protocols for reporting hate crimes. Finally, respondents failed to see how reporting benefited either the victim or the police. In fact, they perceived that they were wasting police time and resources.

In an empirical study incorporating a more representative sampling methodology, Zaykowski (2010) examined victim reporting data from the National Crime Victimization Survey for the years 1992 through 1995 to determine how race influences the likelihood of reporting and the differences between reporting racial and non-racial hate crimes. Her results indicated minority victimizations are less likely to be reported for both racial and non-racial hate crimes. However, the magnitude of underreporting was found to be greater for racial hate crimes compared to non-racial hate crimes which she concluded reflected more nuanced issues associated with reporting practices. The propensity for bias crimes to be relatively underreported was also detected by Pezzella et al. (2019) study of the 2014 NCVS data. The researchers found that bias crimes, compared to non-bias crimes, reflected a clear pattern of underreporting.

The NCVS captures victim's reasons for both reporting and non-reporting (See Table 7.1). Pezzella et al. (2019) assessed reasons why bias crime victims chose to not report using NCVS data from 2010 to 2014. The two most prevalent reasons victims chose not to report were because they reported to another official (22.3%) and perceived the incident as a personal matter (15.6%). Other reasons victims chose not to report including incident unimportant to police (16.7%), police inefficiency (7.5%), and police bias (5%) implicated negative perception of police legitimacy. The researchers suggested their findings support previous research that found an inverse relationship between the perception of police legitimacy and reporting. They noted that negative perceptions of police legitimacy comprised nearly 30% of all the reasons victims chose to not report to police. A careful examination of the nature of these reasons for not reporting implicates poor police-community relations or perhaps less than desirable communication. These reasons coincide with previous theories that perceived police legitimacy and lack of confidence in law enforcement to provide procedural justice influences victim decisions to report crime (Bottoms & Tankebe, 2012; Tyler & Fagan, 2008). So why do hate crime victims report? In the same study, Pezzella et al. (2019) found that the most important reasons victims do report is to stop the incident, prevent future incidents against the victim or others, catch and punish the offender, perceive a duty to tell police, to recover property, needed help, were injured, and to collect insurance.

Summary

Victim underreporting of hate crime is undoubtedly affected by many factors some which are shared with the underreporting of ordinary crimes unrelated to hate motivations. Social, cultural, language, cost-benefit factors, and perception of police legitimacy produce the net effect of substantial underreporting of hate crime victims. In addition, underreporting varies by victim groups. However, victim underreporting does not exclusively explain the impediments to accurately measuring hate crimes. Once victims decide to report, police have the responsibility of classifying the crime as bias motivated where appropriate. The capacity of law enforcement to accurately classify hate crimes is an equally important problem in measurement that have dire consequences reflected in the underestimation of hate crime prevalence.

References

Balboni, J. M., & McDevitt, J. (2001). Hate crime reporting: Understanding police officer perceptions, departmental protocol, and the role of the victim is there such a thing as a "Love" crime? *Justice Research and Policy, 3*(1), 1–27.

Berrill, K. T. (1990). Anti-Gay violence and victimization in the United States: An overview. *Journal of Interpersonal Violence, 5*(3), 274–294.

Berrill, K. T., & Herek, G. M. (1990). Primary and secondary victimization in anti-gay hate crimes official response and public policy. *Journal of Interpersonal Violence, 5*(3), 401–413.

Bottoms, A., & Tankebe, J. (2012). Beyond procedural justice: A dialogic approach to legitimacy in criminal justice. *The Journal of Criminal Law and Criminology*, 119–170.

Bureau of Justice Assistance. (1997). *A policymaker's guide to hate crimes-National Criminal Justice Reference Service*. Retrieved from https://www.ncjrs.gov/pdffiles1/bja/162304.pdf.

Chakraborti, N., & Hardy, S. J. (2015). *LGB&T hate crime reporting: Identifying barriers and solutions*.

Comey, J. (2014). *The FBI and the ADL: Working toward a world without hate, speech at the Anti-Defamation League National Leadership Summit*, Washington DC April 28, 2014.

Fetzer, M. D., & Pezzella, F. S. (2020). Hate crimes: A special category of victimization. In R. Geffner, V. Vieth, V. Naughan-Eden, A. Rosenbaum, L. Hamberger, & J. White (Eds.), *Handbook of interpersonal violence across the lifespan*. Springer.

Fohring, S. (2014). Putting a face on the dark figure: Describing victims who don't report crime. *Temida, 17*(4), 3–18.

Greenberg, M. S., & Beach, S. R. (2004). Property crime victims' decision to notify the police: Social, cognitive, and affective determinants. *Law and Human Behavior, 28*(2), 177–186.

Lim, H. A. (2009). Beyond the immediate victim: Understanding hate crimes as message crimes. *Hate Crimes: The Consequences of Hate Crime, 2*, 107–222.

Martin, S. E. (1996). Investigating hate crimes: Case characteristics and law enforcement responses. *Justice Quarterly, 13*(3), 455–480.

Masucci, M., & Langton, L. (2017). *Hate crime victimization, 2004–2015*. Washington, DC: US Department of Justice, Office of Justice Programs, Bureau of Justice Statistics.

Nicholas, S.,Kershaw, C., & Walker, A (2007). *Crime in England and Wales 2006/07*, Home Office Statistical Bulletin 11/07

Nolan, J. J., & Akiyama, Y. (1999). An analysis of factors that affect law enforcement participation in hate crime reporting. *Journal of Contemporary Criminal Justice, 15*(1), 111–127.

Perry, B., & Alvi, S. (2012). 'We are all vulnerable' the in terrorem effects of hate crimes. *International Review of Victimology, 18*(1), 57–71.

Pezzella, F. S., Fetzer, M. D., & Keller, T. (2019). The dark figure of hate crime underreporting. *American Behavioral Scientist*. https://doi.org/10.1177/0002764218823844

Sin, C. H. (2013). Making disablist hate crime visible: Addressing the challenges of improving reporting. *Disability, Hate Crime and Violence*, 147–165.

Thorneycroft, R., & Asquith, N. L. (2015). The dark figure of disablist violence. *The Howard Journal of Criminal Justice, 54*(5), 489–507.

Tyler, T. R. (1990). *Why people obey the law*. Yale University Press.

Tyler, T. R., & Fagan, J. (2008). Legitimacy and cooperation: Why do people help the police fight crime in their communities. *Ohio State Journal of Criminal Law, 6*, 231–275.

Wong, K., & Christmann, K. (2008). The role of victim decision-making in reporting of hate crimes. *Community Safety Journal, 7*(2), 19.

Zaykowski, H. (2010). Racial disparities in hate crime reporting. *Violence and Victims, 25*(3), 378–394.

Chapter 8
The Law Enforcement Response to Hate Crimes

Abstract This chapter looks at the reasons the law enforcement response to hate crimes has been largely ineffective and the impact this has on the capacity for researchers to accurately measure hate crime. The chapter begins by looking at the magnitude of evidence of law enforcement underreporting. Moreover, the burgeoning number of police agencies that voluntarily participate in the UCR Hate Crime Statistics program is contrasted against the negligible increase in police reported hate crimes over the three decades of the program. The chapter reviews the sequential steps involved in reporting beginning with the victim's decision to report and the first responding police officer's inclination and ability to accurate classify hate crimes. Explanations for law enforcement underreporting including the inability to accurate classify hate crimes at the moment of the criminal incident are covered. Lastly, chapter 8 reviews research that found that police agencies with written hate crime enforcement and reporting policies and formal hate crime training are more likely to report hate crimes.

Keywords Police misclassification of hate crimes · Police underreporting · Hate crime policy · Hate crime training · Bias crime training · Community engagement and hate crime reporting

Despite numerous recommendations to improve enforcement and reporting of hate crimes, it is not an exaggeration to describe the law enforcement response to hate crimes as largely ineffective. Several factors have been found to impede the law enforcement response. State and local laws, politics, the presence of hate crime policies, internal departmental management issues including funding, training, and the level of integration and engagement with the representative community are all relevant factors that influence the law enforcement response to hate crimes. This chapter primarily presents the evidence of problems that preclude an effective law enforcement response to hate crimes.

F. S. Pezzella, M. D. Fetzer, *The Measurement of Hate Crimes in America*, SpringerBriefs in Criminology, https://doi.org/10.1007/978-3-030-51577-5_8

Classification Issues and Law Enforcement Underreporting

Evidence of Law Enforcement Underreporting

To begin, it is important to understand that not all of the approximate 18,500 police agencies participate in the hate crime reporting program (Fetzer & Pezzella, 2020; Pezzella, Fetzer, & Keller, 2019; United States Commission on Civil Rights, 2019). Fetzer and Pezzella's (2020) analysis of participating police agencies in 2016 indicated that of the 18,481 eligible police agencies, only 15,254 or 83% voluntarily participated. Incorporating this same base number of eligible police agencies in 2018, only 16,039 or 86% of police agencies participated in the reporting program (FBI, 2019). The magnitude of the differences in police agency participation rates is more or less the same within a few percentage points throughout the past two decades of the UCR Hate Crime Statistics Program. As a result, the ability to accurately measure hate crime prevalence commences with a statistical disability. That is, approximately 15% of eligible agencies are not reporting hate crime data to the UCR reporting program. Secondly, another major flaw in the reporting of hate crime data concerns the inconsistent reporting practices of participating police agencies. Roy Austin, former Deputy Assistant Attorney General of the Civil Rights Division at the U.S. Department of Justice testified about the negligence of police agencies that do not respond to the FBIs request for hate crime data before the United States Commission on Civil Rights (USCCR) (2019) briefing:

> The numbers currently kept by the FBI...are largely useless. While a small handful of states and law enforcement agencies seem to take the collection of hate crime numbers seriously, the majority of states and the vast majority of law enforcement agencies do not seriously report hate crime numbers. And the handful of numbers that are reported are released late and unaudited...There are approximately 18,000 law enforcement agencies in the United States. And almost 3000 did not even bother to respond to the FBI request for hate crime information. And they suffer no consequences for not doing so (p. 81).

To this point, the USCCR (2019) reported that in 2017, of the more than 18,000 police agencies, 12% did not submit hate crime data. This includes nine cities with populations of over 100,000 – many with over 250,000 citizens. Further, the USCCR report indicated that in 2016 approximately 1500 law enforcement agencies did not report data to the UCR hate crime program and the state of Hawaii has never participated in the FBI's data collection effort since its inception. Similarly, in 2015, geographic areas with histories of racial tension such as Mobile, Alabama and the state of Mississippi did not report their hate crime data to the UCR Hate Crime Statistics Program. In addition, federal agencies have only started reporting hate crimes in 2018 (FBI, 2019).

It is important to understand that these governmental entities did not report zero hate crimes. These municipalities did not respond to the FBI's request for reporting at all. Underreporting is also quite evident within the law enforcement agencies that do participate and report to the UCR program. Pezzella et al. (2019) analyzed two decades of reporting practices by police agencies between 1995 and 2015 and found that 10% of police agencies reported at least one hate crime but an astounding 90% reported "zero" hate crimes each year. Moreover, participating agencies that do report do not necessarily report for all 4 quarters and this includes both agencies that report hate crimes and zero reporting agencies. Pezzella et al. (2019) remarked that these underreporting numbers are even more alarming considering "the number of participating law enforcement agencies has burgeoned from 2771 in 1991 to 14,997 in 2015 representing 93% of the U.S. population" (p. 6). Moreover, they note "the number of statutorily protected groups have also increased" (p. 6). The magnitude of underreporting is displayed in Fig. 8.1 with an examination of trend curves depicting the number of single-bias reported crimes, victims, and participating police agencies over the last 23 years of the UCR hate crime reporting program. As Fig. 8.1 indicates, the number of single-bias reported crimes and victims follow the same basic trends over the 24 previous years of the UCR hate crime reporting program. A total of 5932 single-bias crimes reported in 1994 increased by 1104 to 7036 reported single-bias crimes in 2018 constituting an increase 18%. However, during the same period the number of UCR hate crime reporting police agencies more than doubled. In 1994, 7200 police agencies voluntarily participated in the hate crime reporting program; by 2018, 16,039 police agencies voluntarily participated (FBI, 1994; 2019). Intuitively, one would expect the average number of single bias filings to have increased proportionately with the increase in the rate of participation in police agencies. What explains the negligible increase of single-bias crimes during the same period in which participation by police agencies increased precipitously? An analysis of UCR hate crime crimes by police agencies reveals that

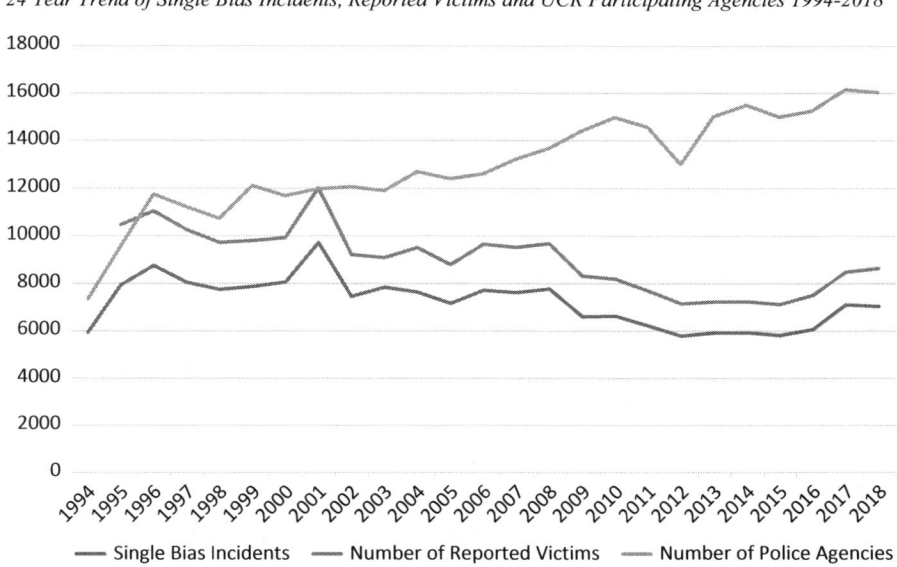

24 Year Trend of Single Bias Incidents, Reported Victims and UCR Participating Agencies 1994-2018

Fig. 8.1 24 Year Trend of Single Bias Incidents, Reported Victims and UCR Participating Agencies 1994–2018

89% of participating police agencies report zero hate crimes each year (Pezzella et al., 2019). This number of police reported single-bias crimes stands in stark contrast to the dark figure of reported hate crimes indicated by the National Crime Victimization Survey (Masucci & Langton, 2017; Pezzella et al., 2019)

The USCCR briefing (2019) illuminates in even greater detail the practice of law enforcement agencies reporting zero hate crimes. The report notes that "for the past several years the majority of law enforcement agencies indicated they had "zero" hate crimes including seventy cities with populations over 100,000" (p. 70). Moreover, "in 2017, nine cities did not report hate crime data to the FBI and over 80 cities reported zero hate crimes to the FBI. Each of these cities has more than 100,000 residents and many have more than 250,00 residents" (p. 70).

The extent of underreporting was also uncovered in an investigation undertaken by the Associated Press (AP). Christina Cassidy (2016), an AP investigative reporter, indicated that "more than 2700 city police and county sheriff's departments across the country which represent about 17 percent of all city and county law enforcement agencies nationwide have not submitted a single hate crime report" to the FBI for the six-year period between 2009 and 2014. The investigation also found that thousands of city police agencies and county sheriff's offices which are responsible for handling the majority of hate crime investigations reported inconsistent data, where they would report for some years, but not others, or only report a quarter of the year. In addition, they revealed there were 16 states where over a quarter of the cities did not appear at all in the UCR database. The investigation also raised serious questions about the internal consistency of the hate crime reporting process in cities where law enforcement officials forward their hate crime statistics to state entities for UCR reporting. The AP investigation noted that law enforcement officials may report accurately and consistently but states may nevertheless report zero hate crimes. Giannasi (2015) argues this may occur because reporting hate crimes "may be counterintuitive for political leaders because they wish to play down the significance of the problems of hate crimes either to protect their reputation or because they do not value the rights of the citizens who are most susceptible to hate crimes or to provide assurance to affected communities" (p. 333). Obviously, these are serious flaws of sizable magnitude that provide indisputable evidence of the reasons for inaccurate estimates of hate crimes. These accounts also explain the dark figure of underreporting (Masucci & Langton, 2017; Pezzella et al., 2019).

Explanations for Law Enforcement Underreporting

What explains the absent or inconsistent reporting practices by law enforcement agencies? There is ample evidence that the first responding police officer's ability or inclination to accurately classify incidents as hate crimes contributes significantly to the problem (Cronin, McDevitt, Farrell, & Nolan, 2007; Fetzer & Pezzella, 2020; Grattet & Jenness, 2008; Levin & McDevitt, 2002; Martin, 1996). Martin's (1996) comparative study of the Baltimore and New York City police departments' processing of bias crimes illuminated the paramount importance of the classification decision by the first responding police officer noting "the ability and willingness [of police officers] requires effective training and clear policies that reward officers for identifying bias cases rather than penalizing them with burdensome workload" (p. 477).

Recall in the previous chapter on victim underreporting the sequential steps outlined as the process that facilitates the reporting and recording of hate crimes (Balboni & McDevitt, 2001; Nolan & Akiyama, 1999). If and when victims decide to report hate crimes, the next step involves the critical role of the first responding police officer to recognize, classify, and record the incident as bias-motivated for later review and reporting to the UCR program (Balboni & McDevitt, 2001; Martin, 1996; Nolan & Akiyama, 1999). However, numerous factors have been found to influence the decision at the point of classification. Typically, the police officer may encounter ambiguous situations where bias is only one of many factors surrounding the criminal incident. As a result, the ambiguity inherent in most criminal incidents with a possible bias motive confounds the officer's understanding of the partial influence of bias motivation. Consequently, the first responding police officer may fail to see a bias motivation (Nolan, McDevitt, Cronin, & Farrell, 2004). Nolan et al. (2004) concurred with prior research that identified "ambiguity in bias crime reporting as both a source of confusion and frustration within law enforcement and as a source of classification error in the national statistics" (p. 93).

Factors unrelated to the bias motivation elements of the criminal incident also influence the officer's classification decision. Heavy caseloads, personal opinions about the tractability of hate crime enforcement, and the officer's perception of the commitment or lack thereof by the police agency has been found related to the first responding officer's classification decision (Fetzer & Pezzella, 2020; Haider-Markel, 2000; Nolan & Akiyama, 1999). The first responding police officer's initial classification decision is the first of many factors that have dire consequences for accurate measurement of hate crimes.

The Importance of Law Enforcement Hate Crime Policy and Formal Training

Findings derived from empirical research have also pointed to the importance of law enforcement agencies having a clear hate crime investigation and enforcement policy (Levin & McDevitt, 2002; Martin, 1996). Hate crime investigation and enforcement policies are important because they send a strong message to victims and police officers. Levin and McDevitt (2002) asserted that the policy requirement of a written report coupled with the supervisor's personal role in the process sends the message "these are indeed serious crimes and are to be treated as a high priority" (p. 161). Martin (1996) also articulated the importance of a written hate crime policy particularly in relation to police departments with a history of insensitivity to ethnic minorities. She asserted "the very existence of a hate crime policy may serve as a vehicle for sensitizing officers and for bridging gaps between the police and the citizens they serve. It also serves as a symbol of the departments affirmative commitment to correct prior biases" (p. 323). Levin and McDevitt (2002) described the primary substance of police department hate crime policies asserting hate crime investigation and enforcement policies should delineate the steps to be taken whenever a possible bias-motivated crime is committed. This includes the person or persons in the police department that should be notified and when. In addition, the policy should include the completion and maintenance of certain records and procedures to be followed up with the victim. Other aspects of police department hate crime policies may include mandatory bias crime training. In fact, some scholars have found that police departments without written hate crime policies are less likely to provide bias crime training, and for the most part, leave it to their officers' discretion to classify incidents as a bias crime (Martin, 1996).

Unfortunately, a plethora of police departments do not have a written hate crime policy (Levin & McDevitt, 2002) and for those that do, often the policy is merely symbolic (Grattet & Jenness, 2008). That is, they exist as the rule of law but are essentially unenforced. Grattet and Jenness (2008) studied the impact of the creation of formal hate crime policies on official reporting practices in 339 municipal police and 58 sheriff's agencies in the state of California over an 8-year period between 1995 and 2002. To facilitate the study, they solicited "general orders" from all of the municipal police and county sheriff's departments. The general orders codified an agency's official policy on hate crimes and provided the departmental hate crime definition and protocol for dealing with hate crimes. They also examined how the effects of community and police agency attributes influence the effects of policy or reporting hate crime. They reported that of the 397 police and sheriff agencies, 39 did not respond to requests for agency policies and 161 (40%) reported they did not have a hate crime policy. Importantly, they found that departments with hate crime policies more than likely reported instrumental effects reflected by enforcement and reporting but these effects were not uniform. Some departments reported hate crime policies that were merely symbolic, but unenforced. Still, they found that when departmental hate crime policies existed, they generally had a positive impact on reporting practices. However, when departmental hate crime policies did not exist, many of these departments had yet to report a single hate crime. Interestingly, they also found that the influence of hate crime policy on reporting varied significantly with the level of integration between law enforcement agencies and the communities they serve. Grattet and Jenness (2008) asserted:

> The more an agency is engaged in a symbiotic relationship with the community in which it resides, the more the policy affects reporting. These findings support the view that hate crime legislation as symbolic laws are not intrinsically incapable of producing changes in enforcement patterns; such effects are dependent upon agency and community processes (p. 518).

Grattet and Jenness' (2008) study provided empirical evidence of the correlations between written hate crime policy, community engagement, and reporting.

Even when hate crime policies were merely symbolic, the level of police-community integration was a better predicter of the likelihood of an instrumental effect of the policy on both enforcement and reporting.

In the absence of a clearly written policy, supported by effective bias crime training, a number of factors have been found to influence the individual officer's classification decision and police agencies reporting practices. Nolan and Akiyama (1999) assessed the factors that affect law enforcement participation in hate crime reporting through a survey of police officers and civilian employees in four police departments representing each region of the United States. They found that the problems that impede law enforcement participation exists at both the police officer level and the agency level. Factors that affect individual police officers' participation in hate crime reporting included: supportive organizational policies and practices including formal and informal systems for recognition and rewards; individual police officer's attitudes and beliefs about hate crime reporting; professional self-preservation conceptualized as the officer's desire to be successful in the police organization; work-related difficulties including obstacles to investigating hate crimes, busy caseloads, and the victim's reticence to assist in prosecution; and the police officer's perception about their organization's commitment to hate crime reporting. Nolan and Akiyama (1999) noted that one measure of commitment is the amount of training resources directed to hate crime investigation and reporting.

Factors that affect police agency participation in hate crimes included shared positive and negative beliefs about hate crime reporting. Importantly, these beliefs included the opinions of citizens about reporting hate crimes in their community, whether they will appreciate the department's hate crime enforcement efforts, whether it is morally right to do so, whether hate crime should be treated as special, perceived usefulness of reporting in community relations, organization self-preservation, efficacy of police involvement in hate crime reporting, and resource for hate crimes. In addition to recommending a formal hate crime training curriculum, Nolan and Akiyama (1999) recommended the following changes to enhance law enforcement participation in hate crime reporting:

1. An organizational policy should be implemented requiring police officers to investigate and take official police reports in all cases where a bias motivation is suspected.
2. Polices should set forth formal, step by step procedures for the investigation and recording of reported hate crimes, the verification of bias motivations, effective strategies for dealing with victims and affected communities, and reporting of verified hate crimes to the UCR program.
3. Policy statements should include explicit statements of value, specifically those relating to the recognition and appreciation of diversity within the jurisdiction and within the police department. These values should be consistent with organizational practices.
4. Police officers who aggressively and effectively investigate hate crimes should be recognized and rewarded for their efforts.

5. Data regarding the occurrence of hate crimes should be shared with community groups at face-to-face meetings between the police and community. This will let the community know that the police are aware that these crimes are occurring, and that they take them seriously.
6. Training and personnel resources for hate crime investigations should remain a priority. Inadequate training and resources in the area of hate crimes sends the message to employees that the program is not a priority (p. 124).

The existence of hate crime policy is a strong predictor of hate crime enforcement and reporting. However, as Grattet and Jenness (2008) detected, the relationship between the two is quite nuanced and other intervening factors may also correlate highly with efficacious reporting.

Cronin et al. (2007) reviewed the reporting procedures and organizational structures in a case study of eight police departments from four separate regions of the United States. In each study site, they collected detailed information on the department's methods for identifying, classifying, and reporting hate crimes to assess characteristics that may affect the completeness and accuracy of hate crime statistics. They found that in each department the role of the first responding police officer was paramount to the initial classification decision. However, the departments differed in subsequent steps in the degree to which they incorporated a specialized process for hate crimes and or the existence of an additional review of the first responding police officer's initial bias classification decision. The researchers noted that the presence or absence of these two fundamental organizational characteristics had implications for the quality of the departments reporting process. With respect to the initial classification decision, they found that ambiguity in determining bias motivation in conjunction with the infrequency in which bias crimes were reported in jurisdictions that required only the first responding police officer to make the decision resulted in potentially fewer bias crimes being reported to state and federal programs. Cronin et al. (2007) recommended several best practices from their comparative case study analysis. First, police departments should train responding officers to apply a broad, inclusive definition of hate crime and identify even suspected hate-motivated crimes. Secondly, departments must implement a second-level review step. The functions of the additional review is important to the effectiveness of the local department's reporting process. Moreover, designated reviewers must be highly trained in hate crime classification for the second-level review to add value to the overall reporting process. They concluded that implementing protocols for identification, investigation, and review may take work on the part of agencies but has the potential to dramatically improve bias-crime reporting.

Walker and Katz (1995) also explained the importance of hate crime training as a reflection of organizational commitment in their study of hate crime units in 16 police departments. First, they reported only half of the police departments provided their police officers with specialized hate crime training. Secondly and more alarming, four departments that reported having an established hate crime unit actually had not. From their analysis of the 16 departments distributed throughout the four regions of the country, they concluded that substantial variation existed in police department's commitment to enforcement of hate crime laws.

The final element of the law enforcement response to hate crimes concerns the enforcement role of the prosecutor. Once police officers have effectively apprehended hate crime offenders and classified the criminal incident as bias-motivated, the enforcement function of state and local district attorneys necessitates prosecuting the case as a bias-motivated crime. However, personal, political, and legal factors often influence whether cases will be prosecuted as a hate crime. The prosecutorial role of local and state district attorneys will be discussed in Chap. 9 where recommendations to enhance the law enforcement response and measurement of hate crimes are presented.

References

Balboni, J. M., & McDevitt, J. (2001). Hate crime reporting: Understanding police officer perceptions, departmental protocol, and the role of the victim is there such a thing as a "Love" crime? *Justice Research and Policy, 3*(1), 1–27.

Cassidy, C. (2016). *AP: Patchy reporting undercuts national hate crimes count.* Associated Press, https://apnews.com/13412889b85640cfb0adcd3c28ad0093.

Cronin, S. W., McDevitt, J., Farrell, A., & Nolan III, J. J. (2007). Bias-crime reporting: Organizational responses to ambiguity, uncertainty, and infrequency in eight police departments. *American Behavioral Scientist, 51*(2), 213–231.

FBI (1994–2019). http://www.fbi.gov/services/cjis/ucr/publications#hate crime statistics.

Federal Bureau of Investigation. (2019). *Hate crime statistics, 2018: About hate crime statistics.* https://ucr.fbi.gov/hate-crime/2018/resource-pages/about-hate-crime.pdf.

Fetzer, M. D., & Pezzella, F. S. (2020). Hate crimes: A special category of victimization. In R. Geffner, V. Vieth, V. Naughan-Eden, A. Rosenbaum, L. Hamberger, & J. White (Eds.), *Handbook of interpersonal violence across the lifespan.* Springer.

Giannasi, P. (2015). The personal injuries of 'hate crime. In *The Routledge international handbook on hate crime* (pp. 331–342). Routledge.

Grattet, R., & Jenness, V. (2008). Transforming symbolic law into organizational action: Hate crime policy and law enforcement practice. *Social Forces, 87*(1), 501–527.

Haider-Markel, D. P. (2000). *Enforcers and activist: The politics of hate crime implementation.* Paper presented at the American Psychological Association conference, Washington, DC.

Levin, J., & McDevitt, J. (2002). *Hate crimes revisited: America's war on those who are different.* Westview Press.

Martin, S. E. (1996). Investigating hate crimes: Case characteristics and law enforcement responses. *Justice Quarterly, 13*, 455–480.

Masucci, M., & Langton, L. (2017). *Hate crime victimization, 2004–2015.* Washington, DC: U.S. Department of Justice, Office of Justice Programs, Bureau of Justice Statistics.

Nolan, J. J., & Akiyama, Y. (1999). An analysis of factors that affect law enforcement participation in hate crime reporting. *Journal of Contemporary Criminal Justice, 15*(1), 111–127.

Nolan, J. J., McDevitt, J., Cronin, S., & Farrell, A. (2004). Learning to see hate crimes: A framework for understanding and clarifying ambiguities in bias crime classification. *Criminal Justice Studies, 17*(1), 91–105.

Pezzella, F. S., Fetzer, M. D., & Keller, T. (2019). The dark figure of hate crime underreporting. *American Behavioral Scientist.* https://doi.org/10.1177/0002764218823844

United States Commission on Civil Rights. (2019). *In the name of hate (Publication No. 11–13)*. Retrieved from https://www.usccr.gov/pubs/2019/11-13-in-the name-of-hate.pdf. Department of Justice, Federal Bureau of Investigation. Hate Crime Statistics, 1994 (Washington, DC: USGPO, 1996), p. 7.

Walker, S., & Katz, C. M. (1995). Less than meets the eye: Police departments bias-crime units. *American Journal of Police, 14*(1), 29–48.

Chapter 9
Recommendations to Improve the Measurement of Hate Crimes

Abstract Based on the issues illuminated throughout the book, Chap. 9 provide recommendations that are designed to overcome the obstacles to measuring and responding to hate crimes. The chapter summarizes recommendations from previous brainstorming sessions from scholars, law enforcement practitioners, civil rights, community, and victims' groups and explains their relevance to the problems that preclude the accurate measurement of hate crimes. The chapter describes the importance of having a written hate crime policy, formal training, improved community engagement, improving hate crime data collection and mandatory reporting, engaging local politicians, tracking non-criminal bias incidents, and enhancing the role of the prosecutor. Chapter 9 concludes with best practices models from several police department around the country and explains why their approach to hate crimes is so effective.

Keywords Hate crime reporting recommendation · Law enforcement hate crime response · Best practice hate crime models · Oak Creek police department · Seattle police department · Written hate crime policy · Hate crime training · Bias crime training · Community engagement · Law enforcement reporting · Tracking non-criminal bias incidents · Enhancing the role of the prosecutor · Mandatory reporting · Incentivizing hate crime reporting

The purpose of writing this book was to explain the problems associated with measuring the nature and prevalence of hate crimes in the United States. We believe that until these problems are corrected, public policies designed to address hate crimes will continue to be an ineffective and inefficient use of resources that cannot reach hate crime victims. We thought the best way to bring the problems to light was to lay out the entire landscape of hate crime offending in the United States. We discussed the history of hate crime legislation, jurisprudence, conceptualization, the strengths and weaknesses of contemporary reporting systems and the difficulties with accurately measuring hate crime. The chapter on patterns and trends delineated

F. S. Pezzella, M. D. Fetzer, *The Measurement of Hate Crimes in America*, SpringerBriefs in Criminology, https://doi.org/10.1007/978-3-030-51577-5_9

our understanding of hate crimes with the existing measurement capacity although we concede conclusions are drawn from flawed reporting systems. We discussed theories and empirical research that explained the uniqueness of hate crimes as the rationale that undergirds contemporary hate crime statutes, policies, and jurisprudence. The chapter on victim underreporting portrayed the first major obstacle to accurate measurement of hate crimes. The chapter summarized the reasons for not reporting and concluded that underreporting results in flawed measurement systems. In Chap. 8 we discussed the law enforcement response to hate crimes by illuminating the pervasive evidence of underreporting by police agencies. Now, after describing the landscape of hate crime, we present recommendations that address critical measurement issues, which we hope will improve estimates of hate crimes in the United States.

Recommendations

Many of the issues that affect the response and measurement of hate crimes were addressed previously by scholars, law enforcement professionals, community, civil rights, and victim advocacy groups in special brainstorming meetings to unpack the problems that have plagued the response to hate crime over the years. More than two decades ago, the International Association of Chiefs of Police (IACP) convened the Hate Crime in America Policy summit that derived 48 recommendations to address enforcement, reporting, and measurement problems associated with hate crimes. Similarly, in 1997, U.S. Department of Justice, Office of Justice Programs, Bureau of Justice Assistance convened a working group of criminal justice professionals including the FBI, the Community Relations Service, the U.S. Department of Treasury's Federal Law Enforcement Training Center, the National Association of Attorneys General, and the International Association of Directors of Law Enforcement Standards and Training to develop hate crime training curricula. Decades later, in response to the recent spike in hate crimes, in 2018, the International Association of Chiefs of Police (IACP) partnered with the Lawyers Committee for Civil Rights under law (LCCRUL) to create the Enhance the Response to Hate Crimes Advisory Committee (ERHCAC). The ERHCAC convened law enforcement practitioners, community and civil rights groups, and academia to discuss the policy and practice problems that obstruct an effective law enforcement response to hate crimes and derive recommendations for promising practices to enhance the response going forward. Lastly, in 2019, the United States Commission on Civil Rights (USCCR) convened a hearing on hate crimes in which scholars, community, civil rights and victim groups, and law enforcement professionals testified about the burgeoning problems with hate crimes.

It is interesting to note that many of the recommendations for enhancing the response to hate crimes are repeated throughout these meetings. Here, we enumerate and explain those recommendations that we think have a simultaneous impact on both the response and measurement of hate crimes. We also discuss best practices employed by police departments around the country.

Written Hate Crime Policy

The importance of law enforcement agencies having a written hate crime policy cannot be overemphasized. In Chap. 7 several of the hate crime scholars discussed the signals it sends to both the public and rank and file police officers (Grattet & Jenness, 2008; Levin & McDevitt, 2002; Martin, 1996). The ERHCAC (2018) recommended that agency hate crime policies be publicized with public awareness campaigns that reflect a community-wide commitment to eliminating hate and intolerance and educates the public on legal protections against hate crimes. Moreover, the advisory committee suggested agencies use social media to publicize policies with hashtags such as #strongerthanhate.

The written hate crime policy should be visibly posted throughout the department and include an explicit statement of value relating to the department's appreciation of diversity and the requirements for police officers to investigate and take official reports where bias motivation is suspected (Nolan & Akiyama, 1999). The written hate crime policy should also delineate procedures for investigation, recording, bias motivation verification, and reporting to the UCR hate crime program. The very existence of a written hate crime policy has been found to increase the probability of reporting to the UCR. However, those that enumerate step-by-step procedures are more likely to ensure that policies are not just "symbolic" but have an "instrumental" effect on enforcement and reporting (Grattet & Jenness, 2008).

Improve Police and Community Engagement

Grattet and Jenness (2008) also found that "the more an agency is engaged in a symbiotic relationship with the community in which it resides, the more the policy affects reporting" (p. 518). To complement written and publicized policies, one of the core recommendations of the ERHCAC was for law enforcement and communities to "work together to help build better community-police relations, foster trust, and encourage hate incident reporting to law enforcement" (p. 5). In Chap. 6, we discussed the problem of victim underreporting and its impact on the enforcement and measurement of hate crimes. If victims are not comfortable with engaging law enforcement, they will not be inclined to report, and their decision will preclude enforcement and accurate measurement of hate crimes. Pezzella, Fetzer, and Keller (2019) found that questions of police legitimacy surrounding bias victims' perceptions of police inefficiency, apathy, and bias constituted 30% of their reasons for not reporting. In essence, police have a public relations problem with many groups within their communities. To this end, several action items were recommended to remove barriers to hate crime reporting. First, law enforcement should identify community leaders that can serve as liaisons to the community for concerns about reporting hate crimes. This could be accomplished by developing a list of community-based organization with points of contact. In addition, law enforcement should participate in community functions to provide informal opportunities for police to engage community member. Police and communities should create formal committees to collaborate on standard operating procedures (SOPS) that delineate how and to whom individuals should report hate incidents and crimes. Collaboratively derived SOPS should be reflected in memorandums of understanding and communicated to citizens and community groups in user-friendly, culturally relevant, and language-sensitive formats. Moreover, the ERHCAC and the IACP summit recommended that communities host regularly scheduled meetings with police to attain feedback on responses to hate crimes, understand the types of hate incidents in the community, and to provide adequate support to victims. These meetings also provide an opportunity for police to share data regarding the occurrence of hate crimes with the community while simultaneously reinforcing that police are seriously engaged in addressing the hate crime problem (Nolan & Akiyama, 1999). We think engagement of this sort will also increase victim reporting.

Track Non-Criminal Bias Incidents

Tracking bias incidents is important as they can evolve into bias crimes (USCCR, 2019). Furthermore, police should keep track of those crimes that they were unable to substantiate bias motivation as well as those that they determine to be hate crimes and those that they rule out. Recognizing the link between non-criminal bias incidents and hate crimes, the 1998 IACP hate crime in America policy summit proposed an extensive plan to track and respond to non-criminal hate incidents. This included training responders to recognize bias-related incidents, encourage bias incident reporting, provide adequate support to victims of hate incidents, ensure swift responses to hate incidents, document incidents thoroughly and consistently, provide community recognition to good samaritans who protect victims of hate incidents, and develop coordinated community incident response plans. The ERHCAC (2018) also recommended that communities report both hate incidents and hate crimes. They reasoned that "identifying where hate incidents occur may help to direct resources to deter and prevent hate crimes" (p. 6). Moreover, they recommended designating an in-house analyst to examine trends in hate incidents. Tracking non-criminal bias incidents will also improve the response to hate crimes indirectly by enhancing the relationship between police and the communities they serve.

Hate Crime Training

The deficit of hate crime training to many scholars and practitioners has been the major obstacle that underlies the ineffective law enforcement response to hate crimes (Haider-Markel, 2002; USCCR, 2019; Walker & Katz, 1995). Both Martin (1996) and Nolan and Akiyama (1999) asserted that the absence of training and resources for hate crimes sends the message to employees that hate crimes are not a priority. Recall the first-responding police officer often encounters ambiguous situations where the bias motivation is not completely apparent (Nolan, McDevitt, Cronin, & Farrell, 2004). The initial bias determination decision is crucial because it is key to the entire bias classification reporting and recording process. Without a flag by the first-responding police officer, the more thorough second stage investigation by specialized bias investigators cannot occur. Hence, the initial bias classification decision is crucial.

Hate crime training is also paramount for other actors in the criminal justice system. According to Nolan and Akiyama (1999) rank and file police officers and police agency managers encourage or discourage enforcement and subsequent processing of hate crimes. Therefore, bias crime training has been recommended for all police officers, including second-stage bias investigators and police management (Martin, 1996; Nolan et al., 2004). In addition, training has been recommended for other actors in the criminal justice system such as victim service providers, prosecutors, and judges (ERHCAC, 2018; IACP, 1999; Wessler, 2000).

Hate crime training programs should be comprehensive and include curricula that covers hate crime offending and victimizations. For law enforcement, both academy and in-service training should be provided for new and experienced police officers. Hate crime curricula should include cultural competence, sensitivity training, and local referral resources for victims (ERHCAC, 2018; USCCR, 2019). Moreover, hate crime investigation training should hone skills in recognizing and responding to potential bias incidents and crimes, determining bias perpetrator's intent, interviewing victims and witnesses, collecting and preserving evidence, completing reporting, and recording documentation and providing relevant information to the prosecutors and courts. The substance of this type of curricula was previously developed pursuant to the Department of Justice (DOJ) 1997 National Hate Crime Training Initiative (Wessler, 2000). The DOJ curricula comprised an 8-hour course that included the history of bias crimes, bias crime identification, definitions, bias indicators, legal issues, effective response guidelines, investigative strategies, collection and preservation of evidence, victim trauma, community strategies and relationships, and case studies. A total of 78 teams derived from "train the trainers" workshops resulted in 31 states receiving more than 138 trainings to more than 4000 law enforcement officers (Wessler, 2000). Unfortunately, this hate crime training program expired for reasons unknown.

Improving Hate Crime Data Collection and Mandatory Reporting

It is important to understand that participation in the UCR Hate Crime Statistics Program is completely voluntary. As noted in Chap. 8, many law enforcement agencies and entire states do not participate, and the majority of those who do report "zero" hate crimes. Moreover, many law enforcement agencies submit incomplete reports providing hate crime data for some quarters but not others. In our opinion, until there are improved incentives to both participate and submit accurate and complete reports to the UCR program, the calculated estimates of hate crimes will continue to lack credibility. This issue was addressed by the USCCR:

> Congress should pass legislation and provide adequate funding that would incentivize local and state law enforcement to more accurately report hate crimes to the FBI, and promote greater transparency and accountability, which would aid in building community trust. Congress should also pass legislation to ensure that federal law enforcement agencies collect and report their hate crime data to the FBI and that states are accurately reporting hate crime data they receive from local law enforcement agencies in their jurisdiction. The federal government should require, as a condition for federal funding, that state and local law enforcement agencies report their data to the FBI, publish data on a quarterly basis, undergo data auditing for accuracy, and work with affinity groups to report hate crimes to the federal government even if a victim does not want to prosecute (p. 226).

However, it should be noted that one such effort towards improving incentives that will impact reporting commenced in 2018. To facilitate the FY 2021 planned replacement of the Summary Reporting System (SRS) with National Incident Based Reporting System (NIBRS), the Bureau of Justice Assistance (BJA) is now requiring that Justice Assistance Grant award (JAG) recipients that are not certified by their state as NIBRS compliant, dedicate 3% of their JAG award towards achieving full compliance with the FBI's NIBRS data submission requirements under the UCR program (BJA, 2018). This requirement will not only ensure that state and local jurisdiction award recipients continue to have critical criminal justice funding, but will increase the likelihood the rich NIBRS data infrastructure is in place to provide consistent reporting for both bias and non-bias motivated crimes.

The ERHCAC also recommended converting to NIBRS and "strengthening data collection, reporting and analysis" with action items that communicate with local government representative the importance of adequate funding and support of local law enforcement agencies in the collection and reporting of hate crime data (p. 5). Likewise, the IACP hate crime policy summit recommended that all agencies identify and report all bias related incident accurately and completely.

Engage State and Local Politicians

Engaging state and local politicians regarding the problem of underreporting is paramount because increased reporting may appear as though it is an uptick in hate crimes when it is actually a product of improved reporting (ERHCAC, 2018). Giannasi (2015) asserted increased reporting may be perceived by local and state politicians to cast a negative light on their community, and consequently they may not support law enforcement request for resources funding to improve reporting. It is important to note that for many state and local officials, hate crime implementation efforts exist within a context of competition with political opponents (Haider-Markel, 1998). Understanding these potentially undermining forces, the ERHCAC recommended communities and law enforcement working together "publicly support agencies that improve hate incident and hate crime reporting especially if local officials are concerned that a reported increase in these incidents would be misinterpreted and reflect poorly on the community" (p. 5). The opinions of state and local politician are also important because their influence on hate crime enforcement policy will also bear on local district attorney's inclination to aggressively prosecute hate crimes (Haider-Markel, 2002).

Enhance the Role of the Prosecutor

The prosecutor's response to hate crime is also vitally important to the perception of how serious law enforcement considers hate crimes. According to the recent USCCR (2019) report "there is general consensus among the American public that a person's civil rights should be protected, but in practice, enforcement of hate crime laws has been unequal and troubling" (p. 44). However, a plethora of personal, political, and legal factors influence whether cases will be prosecuted as a hate crime (Byers, Warren-Gordon, & Jones, 2012). Open Society's senior attorney Marguerite Angelari's testimony before the USCCR explained the divergence between consensus and practice asserting "the same prejudices that motivate people to commit hate crime may also influence the decisions of prosecutors and the actions of police" (USCCR, p. 44). In addition, Grattet and Jenness (2008) asserted when hate crime statutes are largely symbolic, prosecutors have little incentive to take on the added burden of prosecuting hate crimes. Still, local district attorneys are more likely to prosecute hate crimes if a hate crime policy is in place and community support is apparent (Haider-Markel, 2002). However, in 1999, American Prosecutors Research Institute (APRI) noted that most prosecutors' offices do not have written policies on handling hate crimes (Wessler, 2000). To meet that need, the APRI developed a 100 pages resource guide that included chapters on working with outside organizations, case screening and investigation, case assignment and preparation, victim and witness impact support, trial preparation, sentencing alternatives, and prevention efforts.

Prosecution is a key component in the response to hate crimes. The ERHCAC recommended "enhancing the role of prosecutors with early and ongoing communication with law enforcement, proactive engagement with community, development of hate crime expertise" (p. 1). In addition, two of the recommendations from the IACP summit (1999) was for prosecutors to be included as key members in hate crimes taskforce when hate crimes surge in local communities and receive bias crime training.

Best Practices

The Oak Creek Police Department's (OCPD) hate crime response model has been heralded as one of the best (The Police Chief, 2018). OCPD requires officers to attend a broad training curriculum that includes regular updates on hate crime case law. Moreover, experienced officers are required to take in-service training where they learn to investigate and document incidents thoroughly so prosecutors can determine whether an enhanced penalty can be applied. Outreach to the community is an important aspect of OCPD's community engagement activities. Among other police-community activities, OCPD works with potential hate crime victim groups if they request to conduct security surveys and develop security plans. An important characteristic of OCPD training and community engagement is the philosophy of respect for officers and community members. The on-going trainings address how to treat people with respect. OCPD developed the following guiding principles for engaging the community:

- Prioritize education and training for officers.
- Be proactive about reaching out and developing positive relationships with different cultural groups in the community.
- Maintain a visible leadership role in the aftermath of a hate crime or any public safety crisis.
- Be transparent and share as much information about an incident as the department can without jeopardizing an investigation.
- Maintain a strong relationship with the media; "No comment" does not get you anywhere.
- Be approachable-agree to meet with anyone in the community.
- Establish a standard of meaningful community engagement that encourages resident to bring new idea.
- Thoroughly investigate and accurately report every incident that might be a hate crime.
- Recognize that the police department is a community itself, and prioritize community wellness (The Police Chief, p. 10–12).

According to the USCCR (2019) other police departments have also implemented best practices. The Seattle Police Department trains all officers to investigate crimes for bias elements and refer potential bias crimes to a bias crime coordinator for special review. In addition to maintaining and producing statistical reports on hate incidents and crimes, they conduct outreach to multiple communities, identify non-criminal bias incidents, develop programs for targeted communities, share hate crime data with communities, and aid in prosecution of cases. Similarly, the Columbus Police Department (CPD) employed best practices including requiring officers to: report ambiguous hate crime situations to a special detective for a more thorough bias investigation, undergo academy and in-service training to learn how to document hate crime incidents, and collect relevant information for prosecutions. In addition, CPD educates community groups about hate incidents and crimes and meets with community groups upon request to discuss crime and safety topics. The Boston and New York City police departments established specific bias crime units that have the exclusive purpose of focusing on hate crimes. Both departments compile and report hate crime statistics annually. In addition, Massachusetts instituted a hate crime taskforce and requires every police department designate a civil rights officer. Finally, the Phoenix Police Department (PPD) tracks bias incidents because trends show that bias crimes occur where non-criminal bias incidents are reported. PPD also has a specialized bias crime unit with officers specifically trained who lead hate crime investigations and work with victims and community members.

The policies and best practices of these police department undoubtedly enhance the response to hate crimes and serve as models for the majority of the approximate 18,500 police departments in the United States. We think that the improved reporting and classification capacity in these best practice models will also improve our ability to accurately measure hate crimes.

Summary

Taken together, these recommendations would vastly improve the hate crime response, reporting, and measurement system presently in place. However, we believe there are a number of other recommendations that would also aid the response to hate crimes and improve measurement. For instance, standardizing definitions of bias motivations and criminal offenses would perhaps alleviate the ambiguity encountered by the-first responding police officer at the moment of the criminal incident (Nolan et al., 2004). Recall, Cronin, McDevitt, Farrell, and Nolan (2007) recommended a more inclusive definition of bias crime be used so that the final classification could be made by the second-stage officer. They believed that incorporating a more inclusive definition would be beneficial because bias crimes would be less likely to be omitted.

We also believe that measuring multiple units of analysis would also be helpful towards improving our capacity to accurately measure hate crimes. To this end, we concur with the ERHCAC (2018) recommendation that all police departments convert to the National Incident-Based Reporting System. We believe that multiple units of analysis from incident-level data would make it easier to calculate and compare reports from different sources. For instance, NIBRS includes more criminal offenses than presently provided for in the SRS. It provides a rich reservoir of data on victim, offender, and situational characteristics. Moreover, NIBRS data on arrests create the potential for linking bias crime clearance and conviction rates. This would provide another level of understanding of the extent to which the criminal justice system executes the letter and spirit of hate crime policy.

References

Bureau of Justice Assistance. (2018). *Edward Byrne Justice Assistance Grant (JAG) program fact sheet*. https://bja.ojp.gov/sites/g/files/xyckuh186/files/publications/2018-JAG-Fact-Sheet.pdf.

Byers, B. D., Warren-Gordon, K., & Jones, J. A. (2012). Predictors of hate crime prosecutions: An analysis of data from the national prosecutor's survey and state-level bias crime laws. *Race and Justice, 2*(3), 203–219.

Cronin, S. W., McDevitt, J., Farrell, A., & Nolan III, J. J. (2007). Bias-crime reporting: Organizational responses to ambiguity, uncertainty, and infrequency in eight police departments. *American Behavioral Scientist, 51*(2), 213–231.

Enhance the Response to Hate Crime Advisory Committee. (2018). https://www.theiacp.org/sites/default/files/201904/IACP_Hate%20Crimes_Action%20Agenda.pdf.

Giannasi, P. (2015). The personal injuries of 'hate crime'. In *The Routledge international handbook on hate crime* (pp. 331–342). Routledge.

Grattet, R., & Jenness, V. (2008). Transforming symbolic law into organizational action: Hate crime policy and law enforcement practice. *Social Forces, 87*(1), 501–527.

Haider-Markel, D. P. (2002). Regulating hate: State and local influences on hate crime law enforcement. *State Politics & Policy Quarterly, 2*(2), 126–160.

Haider-Markel, D. P. (1998). The politics of social regulatory policy: State and federal hate crime policy and implementation effort. *Political Science Quarterly, 51*(1), 69–88.

International Association of Chiefs of Police. (1999) *Hate crime in America policy summit*, www.theiacp.org/pubinfo/Research/hateamer.htm.

Levin, J., & McDevitt, J. (2002). *Hate crimes revisited: America's war on those who are different*. Westview Press.

Martin, S. E. (1996). Investigating hate crimes: Case characteristics and law enforcement responses. *Justice Quarterly, 13*, 455–480.

Nolan III, J. J., McDevitt, J., Cronin, S., & Farrell, A. (2004). Learning to see hate crimes: A framework for understanding and clarifying ambiguities in bias crime classification. *Criminal Justice Studies, 17*(1), 91–105.

Nolan, J. J., & Akiyama, Y. (1999). An analysis of factors that affect law enforcement participation in hate crime reporting. *Journal of Contemporary Criminal Justice, 15*(1), 111–127.

Pezzella, F. S., Fetzer, M. D., & Keller, T. (2019). The dark figure of hate crime underreporting. *American Behavioral Scientist*. https://doi.org/10.1177/0002764218823844

ThePoliceChiefMagazine.(2018).*Oakcreek:Leadingacommunityintheaftermathofatragedy*.http://www.policechiefmagazine.org/oak-creek-leading-a-community-theaftermath-of-a-tragedy.

United States Commission on Civil Rights. (2019). *In the name of hate (Publication No. 11–13)*. Retrieved from https://www.usccr.gov/pubs/2019/11-13-in-the name-of-hate.pdf.

Walker, S., & Katz, C. M. (1995). Less than meets the eye: Police departments bias-crime units. *American Journal of Police, 14*(1), 29–48.

Wessler, S. (2000). *Addressing hate crimes: Six initiatives that are enhancing the efforts of criminal justice practitioners*. U.S. Department of Justice, Office of Justice Programs, Bureau of Justice Assistance.

Index

123

F. S. Pezzella, M. D. Fetzer, *The Measurement of Hate Crimes in America*,
SpringerBriefs in Criminology, https://doi.org/10.1007/978-3-030-51577-5

Druck:
Customized Business Services GmbH
im Auftrag der
KNV Zeitfracht GmbH
Ein Unternehmen der Zeitfracht - Gruppe
Ferdinand-Jühlke-Str. 7
99095 Erfurt